THE *GILES* FAMILY

Also by Peter Tory

Giles: A Life in Cartoons

THE GILES FAMILY:

THE ILLUSTRATED HISTORY OF BRITAIN'S BEST-LOVED FAMILY

PETER TORY

HEADLINE

First published in 1993
by HEADLINE BOOK PUBLISHING LTD

10 9 8 7 6 5 4 3 2

The photographs in this book have been supplied by courtesy of
Express Newspapers plc and Joan and Carl Giles,
with the exception of p. 70.

British Library Cataloguing in Publication Data

Tory Peter
  Giles Family
  I. Title
  741. 5

ISBN 0 -7472 - 0860 - 3 (hardback)
ISBN 0 7472 7881 4 (softback)

Designed by Penny Mills

Illustration reproduction by Koford, Singapore

Printed and bound in Great Britain by
BPC Hazell Books Ltd
A member of
The British Printing Company Ltd

HEADLINE BOOK PUBLISHING LTD
A Member of the Hodder Headline PLC Group
Headline House
79 Great Titchfield Street
London W1P 7FN

For Mum

Acknowledgements

I would like to thank Joan and Carl Giles for their continuing hospitality and Mark Burgess again for his research.

Contents

THE GILES FAMILY

CHAPTER ONE

The Birth of the Family

In Japan, the Allies were about to drop the atom bomb on Hiroshima and Nagasaki. World War Two was all but over.

In England, on the morning of 5 August 1945, a family was setting out for the seaside. They looked ordinary enough at first glance. We would have known them, recognised their type, just about anywhere in suburban England. We would merely have given them a brief look and continued about our business.

But this lot required closer study. For had we been picnicking on a grassy slope, looking out over some valley amid the folds of the English countryside our attention would have been drawn to this small group walking – yes, walking – along the railway line. The trains, of course, were few and erratically scheduled because of wartime disruption. The railways, then as now, always found an excuse. But it was unusual, just the same, to see a holiday-bound family resort to the questionably logical and startlingly unorthodox measure of taking to the tracks and following them, on Shanks's pony, to their destination. After all, they were only going for the day.

Still, we weren't to know at that stage what we know now. For this was the Giles Family. We hadn't met them before, though we recognised their breed, and we couldn't possibly have known on this sunny August morning that, before very long, they were to become just about the most famous family in the land. In a sense, over the years, they became the First Family, a kind of Royalty. They were to offer a post-war reassurance, a feeling of timeless Englishness, an indestructibility.

Thus, in the late summer of 1945, they made their debut in Gilesland, a bright place which had been created in the *Sunday Express* during the dark days of war by the already immensely popular cartoonist, Carl Giles. A collection of Giles's celebrated characters of that time – taxi drivers, blimpish landowners taking in children from the cities, nurses, GIs and, of course, the mighty, evil protagonists themselves, the comically depicted Hitler and Mussolini – had dominated the war years.

Now, the Giles Family were to dominate peacetime. Indeed, they were to make regular, always acclaimed and joyfully welcomed appearances, reflecting the passing years without themselves growing a fraction of a day older, in both the *Sunday* and the *Daily Express,* three times a week, for the next half a century. This book will follow their adventures.

But let us look quickly again at this first, significant Family outing. Who are they all? How are they related? It cannot have been clear to those readers of the *Sunday Express* on that first Sunday morning.

13

It's quicker by rail.

Sunday Express, Aug. 5th, 1945

This was it! This was the Family's debut. They had always been somewhere out there, of course, in what is known as Little England. But this occasion was the first time they had wandered into the frame of a Giles cartoon. They were never to know how famous they were to become.

Giles said he needed them, on a regular weekly basis, to replace his wartime favourites: Hitler and, in particular, Mussolini. Only Grandma, who could have been either, would have seen the significance of such an exalted notion.

"As usual we all made plans for Easter ...

and as usual, only Mother's came to anything!"

Daily Express, April 16th, 1949

And here they are – the full cast. From left to right below are: Grandma, Carol, Bridget, Ann with her illegitimate twins, George Junior (he doubled as the cartoonist's illiterate spokeschild, Giles Junior, when Giles was indisposed), Vera, George the bookworm, Ernie, Father, *Randy the fish (long swum away) – and Mother, shown in an uncharacteristically tyrannical pose.*

Natalie the Cat follows an early, unnamed, Giles dog into the house. Eventually the Airedale, Butch, was to establish himself as the permanent Family pet.

"I'll tell you what I think about Bank Holidays by the sea."

Daily Express, May 27th, 1975

Anyone who has visited an English beach will sympathise with this back-garden ordeal. Butch the Airedale is seen here as a puppy. There was a succession of real Butches in the Giles's household in Suffolk.

They died, as dogs do, though all of natural causes. Over fifty years within the cartoon world, they were simply reincarnated to become a permanent feature in Gilesland.

The characters were, after all, simply a family group whom they'd never seen before. We know now that the Family was, at that stage, incomplete. There are the twins, their mouths shrieking caves of horrible sound, being pushed by Mother, a sturdy though not particularly large lady wearing a wide-brimmed summer hat and a floral frock.

Whose children are they? Mother is actually Grandmother, we were eventually to discover, and the ferocious lady in the rear, the frightening figure in

"You'll have to take it off Grandma—Butch doesn't like it!"

Sunday Express, July 26th, 1981

Here, the Family react to Grandma's outfit for the Royal wedding of the Prince of Wales and Diana Spencer, on 19 July 1981. A monster in many ways, Grandma was a great Royalist and patriot. Still, she wasn't to know that the marriage – a union described by the Archbishop of Canterbury as 'the stuff of which fairy tales are made' – was to end in disaster. For all her pleasure in strife, she would have been appalled at this outcome.

Note the figure with the camera. He is Stinker, not a Family member but a friend of George Junior's. The most mysterious of all the characters in Gilesland, he never speaks. He only observes, and takes photographs.

"Grace Kelly's got one thing at her wedding I'm glad I didn't have at mine—you in a top-hat."

Daily Express, April 11th, 1956

Giles was invited to the Monaco wedding of actress Grace Kelly and Prince Rainier. He decided to take the Family with him.

While at the nuptials in Monte Carlo – an occasion he obviously saw as preposterous – Giles found himself missing his wife, Joan.

black bombazine, is Great-grandmother, though nowadays we don't know her as that, of course.

She is, of course, Grandma. Grandma, family martinet, rebel, slayer of traffic wardens, rider of motor-cycles, horsewoman, punter, anarchist, con-woman, plotter, drinker of Guinness, merciless prankster and suburban tyrant. Unknown then, she became almost as celebrated and loved, though for rather different reasons, as the Queen Mother herself.

18

"Grandma, forty cigarettes a day for the last sixty-odd years haven't done you any harm—why change now?"

Sunday Express, March 11th, 1962

Here is a rare reference to age, a subject which is seldom addressed in the world of Giles. Time stands still, surely.

How old is Grandma? When did she start smoking? At 2? At 59? At 160? We will never know the answer.

THE GILES FAMILY TREE

Mother's husband – Father, quite naturally – leads the pack here. A bag containing thermos and sandwiches is hanging from his left hand and the hideous baby, George Junior, dummy stuffed into his mouth, is taking a ride on Father's right arm. Another youngster on this first Family sighting is Ernie. Spotty and determined, shoulders hunched with a grim sense of imminent, sand-castle destiny, he is already betraying the Family likeness in his features. There is an unidentifiable kid tumbling down the bank as a little girl – pig-tailed Bridget maybe, one of the three Giles Family sisters – looks on. A small creature holds up its paws in alarm.

We will meet the rest of them soon. But as we watch the progress of the Giles Family down the railway line, it might be worth asking where they came from. What inspired their creation? Which of the unwitting characters that filled the colourful and happy childhood of the artist were to be the models for these strange people who combine recognisable ordinariness with alarming eccentricity?

Giles explains:

All my work for the *Express* up until then had been in the wartime. All the characters were wartime characters – or people caught up in the war. Suddenly they were gone. I had lost them – Hitler, Mussolini – disreputable little Franco was still there, of course – Himmler, Goering, Goebbels. I remember writing to my wife, Joan, from Europe where I was a war correspondent. At the end of the letter there was a PS which said: 'I've just lost my best character, Musso.' I drew the Family as something which could take their place. After that, whenever I couldn't think of anything else I fell back on the Family.

So how did the Family fare in the war? There is no record of their participation but there is, intriguingly, some evidence that they did not entirely lack some kind of involvement.

We have never been told, for example, who was the father of the twins, Ralph and Laurence (named, incidentally, after Sir Ralph Richardson and Sir Laurence Olivier). Daughter Ann, who along with her sister Carol did not join that first seaside picnic, is undoubtedly the long-suffering mother. But of the father, never a mention.

Giles fans who read this book are now about to share a secret which has been kept for half a century. The facts have long been known by a select few and Grandma, not known for her sense of discretion, was almost certainly aware of it. The other Family members had long suspected it.

However, here it is from someone who, surely, is in a better position than most to know all the uncomfortable facts. Says Giles:

Oh, yes. It was an American serviceman. No doubt at all. They never spoke about it, but most of them knew. But then girls in those days, after the war, didn't speak about things like that. It was peace – things were different – and they just got on with it. You have to remember that there were a great number of babies after the war whose fathers were back in America. Many of them didn't even know. You often had to wait for the babies to sit up in the pram to see their colour – many were black, some of them were Chinese. When you considered the ethnic mix in the US forces you could expect just about anything.

Giles is entertained by the anarchy of his world. Indeed, the prevailing theme of most of his work is mischief of some kind or another. This is nowhere more evident than in the youngsters, the celebrated ruffians and malevolent mites who attach fireworks to the cat, who shoot arrows at the huge backside of the neighbouring lady as she tends her prize marrow, who roll a spiky-haired sprog in a barrel down a cobbled hill into the midst of the Saturday morning market, who ambush angelic-faced choirboys with snowballs, who use a catapult on the traffic warden. Giles's work bustles with young menaces, hooligans who then, as now, seem to be permanently above and beyond the law of the land.

The Giles Family lads and their friends, with the twins as mute and malevolent witnesses, are always in the thick of it.

Where did Giles himself receive such a merry, yet jaundiced view of youth? We do not have to look far.

As a youngster, Giles seemed to combine an outstanding creative talent with that of a young villain. Perhaps not an outright villain, but certainly a lad who was not averse to the pleasure of a certain degree of torment and torture.

His sister Eileen, who is six years younger, was a principal victim. Giles would wind all her fluffy toys and painting tubes through their mother's mangle. They came out completely flattened.

When Giles took to the streets to play with his gang, the young lass would toddle along after him. Giles, determined that her presence would not interfere with his fun, would place her on top of a red letter-box. Eileen was incapable of letting herself down. She would sit there, clutching a flattened teddy bear, in mute terror.

And she would certainly never complain.

Explains Giles, still tremendously amused by the recollection: 'I told her that I was a friend of God's. And that if she told our mother about me, God would let me know. The poor mite was petrified.'

So it is not difficult to see where Giles did his research. He was also a member of a class which was presided over by the frightening schoolmaster, Chalkie. Chalkie – or Mr Chalk, as he was named – was the only human character who was drawn, with as much ill-natured accuracy as Giles could muster, from reality.

In that class there were evidently memorable characters who, through fear, ruled the playground and the surrounding streets.

'One of them was Georgie Smith and the other was Arthur Elkington,' recalls Giles, who was a short-haired, bespectacled kid not noted for a muscular frame or a way with his fists.

'They were fighters. You can tell, by the look of them, even now in the school photograph. Arthur was a big bloke with sideburns. Nobody got into a scrap with him. Yet he took it as an offence if you didn't have a go at 'im. You couldn't win either way. He was lean and tough. Actually, I rather liked him. In the end he became my minder. No one would hit me while I was with him. I was very proud of the fact that I had been accepted by a bloke like Elkington.'

This is Giles's sister, Eileen. She poses uncertainly on a chair for the photographer. If Giles himself had been present it would account even more for her look of apprehension. She was persistently tormented by her older brother and had to endure the horror of having all her teddy bears and dolls being wound through the family wringer.

Despite all, the two have always adored each other. Giles, to this day, calls her 'mate'.

Giles was asked at this stage whether he was, in any sense, what might be regarded as a force to be reckoned with.

'If I could find a little cripple,' he replied, the sun catching his glasses at his position in his wheelchair by the French windows at his Suffolk farm, 'I'd go slog him round the ear. But he'd have had to have his leg in irons.'

So it is not surprising, really, that the youth of the Giles Family behaves as it does. It is the young and the aged – the aged in the form of Grandma, of course – who are the monsters. More of Grandma in a later chapter, but what can we say of Father and Mother? In Gilesland this pair represent the decent, conscientious couple who have long since abandoned all hope of creating order out of chaos. They are phlegmatic characters, noble even, who cope without complaining and somehow keep the Family together. They exist in the middle of an appallingly unruly world and somehow, by their presence and their dedication to domestic order, prevent it from falling apart. They are the hero and heroine of the Giles Family, yet remain unsung, and undeservedly so. For them, no fame or notoriety. Just the satisfaction that they are doing – have done – their duty. England – little England – expects it.

Giles's childhood was enormously happy. His own household, a well-ordered place where discipline and love prevailed in an admirable but rare balance, was very different from the household of his creation.

When young Giles went out into the Islington streets to play with his chums, he was invariably followed by his worshipping sister, Eileen. Inconvenienced by her toddling presence, he would place her on the nearest scarlet pillar-box. She was unable to get down, of course, and would remain there, in mute terror, threatened by her brother with the intervention of God.

However, the placid, decent natures of his fictional Father and Mother reflect the great respect he had for his own.

'They were lovely people,' says Giles.

They were quiet and decent and loving. My father was a popular man who didn't say much, but when he did he could be very funny. He ran a couple of tobacconists' shops in Islington and the Barbican, and all his friends would go in there and treat the place as a club. They would stand around these great big black barrels of tobacco which were in a line in front of the counter and gossip. There would be wonderful smells, smells from all over the world. My father would be silent for a long time, then he would say something quietly and they would all roar with laughter.

While Giles's high regard for his own mother is echoed in the calm dignity of the Family Mother, his more personal, fond recollections of the lady would make less than suitable subjects for publication in the cartoon.

'I remember when Eileen was born,' said Giles, recalling those days in 1922 before the fireplace in Islington. 'My mother would be breast-feeding her and

Giles poses with his schoolmates for the class photograph. He is the figure who looks startlingly like a youthful Jack Kennedy, the late US President, third from the left in the top row. Giles was no good with his fists in the playground, but was in awe of those who were – such as Georgie Smith and Arthur Elkington.

He says that they were the sort who were offended if you didn't take them on. You couldn't win, recalls Giles. Hit them and you'd had it, avoid them and you'd had it too. That's the way it was, in all playgrounds.

I would howl the place down because I couldn't have the other one. I used to resent this priority always given to my little sister. My mother used to fight me off – my father used to be called in to pull me away.'

Along with the daughters Ann and Carol, who were the other Family members who had apparently found something better to do on that August day in 1945, George, Father's bookish eldest son, and Vera,

24

'Cor,' says Giles. 'Don't I look bloody awful. Then and now. In every picture. 'Orrible.'

Giles holds his baby cousin.

his snuffling, snivelling, hypochondriac wife, are two who only appear later.

The thin, bespectacled Vera, always visiting the chemist's shop for pills and potions, expectorants and unguents, drops and mixtures, or gargles and lozenges, is an auntie figure who seems to be a combination of all kinds of clearly remembered, permanently suffering ladies from Giles's youth.

'You basically identify Vera with aspirins,' he says.

'You always remember women like that from your childhood who were taking aspirins – for everything, it seemed.

'But they were also women who smelt of surgeries. Wintergreen ointment, I remember, was a particularly powerful smell. And whenever they went past you would smell other things – embrocation and camphorated oil.'

Vera, it will be noticed, always takes the pill bottle

back to be refilled.

'That's what I used to have to do,' recalls Giles. 'Take empty pill bottles back for filling up by the chemist. It was always for aunts. No one else.'

All of it means or matters little to Vera's husband, George. There are three Georges in the Giles Family. George known as the bookworm wears a beret and smokes a meerschaum pipe. He has his long, angular nose permanently pressed into a volume or treatise of, we must presume, a philosophical nature. His pipe is never lit and we never see him turn a page. Mayhem and catastrophe swirl about him and he never so much as lifts his eyes from the prose.

There are cartoons which show him on safari, with bull elephants charging and rhinos about to trample Grandma. George, pipe in mouth, beret on head, remains impervious and unmoved, still and tranquil, his thoughts transfixed by the printed word.

'Well, there were those intellectual Hampstead types – they were all like that,' says Giles. 'They all wore berets and smoked pipes. But I suppose the nearest character to George that I knew was Monty Slater. He was very much like George in character, if in no other way.'

Slater was a columnist and commentator on Giles's first newspaper, the cooperative-owned, communist *Reynolds News*. He is best known as the librettist for Benjamin Britten's opera, *Peter Grimes*.

He was an influential figure in Giles's life, for he lured the artist close to communism. Giles would spend much time in his company, in wine bars behind Fleet Street, listening to his quietly expressed, earnest philosophies. Giles had never met such a man, not in his schooldays nor in his apprenticeship as a film animator.

George, however comical he may appear in the midst of the Giles Family madness, is an interestingly pensive presence, always to one side of events, always silent, but always there.

Another figure on the sidelines, a character who is not strictly Family but who is seldom absent, is Stinker, the spiky-haired little boy who observes through a camera – almost voyeuristically – everything that occurs.

It is often interesting to follow the line of his lens in any particular cartoon in order to discover what Giles himself finds most interesting. Like all good photographers, Stinker always sees what is about to transpire and manages to get himself in the best possible position to capture the drama. You will most certainly never find him snapping a sunset or the first glimpse of blossom outside the Family's home.

Nor will he be much interested in taking pictures, at the Family's local church, of suburban brides.

He will always be lurking, like a hard and ruthless newspaper photographer, around the location most likely to produce drama, tragedy or disaster. He will note that Ernie has attached a rope to a post which temporarily supports a ledge upon which there is a large open tin of white emulsion. Grandma will be snoozing below, the racing pages open on her lap.

No one else is aware of the approaching horror except Stinker. It would not occur to him to call a warning, of course; instead, he merely adjusts his focus so that he can photograph with supreme clarity the moment that the can topples, inverted, and crashes about Grandma's ears. There is something truly malevolent about Stinker. For it is one thing to engineer mischief, and quite another to wish to keep a record of it. Wherever his little bedroom is, it must be full of files and photographs of an unspeakably horrid nature: a pictorial history of accidents and of pain. It may well be that Stinker includes, on his bookshelves, volumes by the Marquis de Sade and the annotated histories of serial murders and of medieval torture methods in the Tower of London.

"Another war in the Far East—I thought Errol Flynn had stopped all that."

Daily Express, June 27th, 1950

The Korean War breaks out and Vera is terrified. Here is the malevolence of Giles at its best. And it needs a second look at the cartoon to see it at work. This pathetic, scrawny woman is about to have the vapours over a distant conflict, with all its death and destruction, and Ernie is on the point of rudely relieving her of her chair, an act which – as those who have played such tricks will know – can cause quite serious injury. Vera, poor woman, receives no compassion from anybody. Grandma, in the next, unseen, frame of this sequence, will be barking with laughter.

But not according to Giles.

'I like him. I got to like him more and more,' says the artist. 'He was a favourite in a way. He became very important. The funny thing is that he was called Stinker in the cartoons but the readers started to write in and call him Larry. Independently. I don't know why, but I suppose it was rather a suitable name.

'He's a friend of George Junior who has attached himself to the Family,' says Giles. 'Like a lot of such friends, no one is quite sure who his parents are or exactly where his home is. He's just always in the house. Or around George. Whatever George is up to, you'll find him there.'

He is more than that, however. For he never speaks. He has never uttered a word. He has never been given, as Giles explains, 'a caption'. And that really is strange – a little boy who is eternally silent and takes photographs. On the other hand he is the only character in the ensemble who shows any creative talent. Any drive, indeed. If they were all released from their timeless, ageless state one feels that young Stinker would soon leave suburbia, forget the Family, find quick employment as an apprentice to a celebrated photographer and one day become a figure of renown. Just like Giles.

So where does Stinker come from? We will never know. Still, here is another first which readers of this book will be able to make use of at their leisure. He was the inspiration – and it is a theory which is not denied by his creator – for the whole of the punk movement. Just as the tiny beat of a butterfly's wings can cause an eddy that causes a swirl that causes a wind that causes a storm that causes a hurricane, so it was that the first appearance of Stinker, with his electric-shock, inky-black spiky hairdo, caused, in time, the worldwide youth phenomenon which so alarmed and frightened the older generation.

That's our story and we're sticking to it.

There has been another puzzle for readers: the mystery and confusion over the identity of the second of Mother and Father's three daughters. The three girls are Ann, Bridget and Carol. That was the order in which they were originally created and that, going by the evident difference in their ages, was also – out of frame and before the Giles Family had ever been heard of – their order of birth.

Ann is the mother of the illegitimate twins (the father, as we have surmised, was most likely a GI). Bridget is the lass, a little younger, who wears tight jumpers and jeans and who is usually seen prettifying herself. It is she who often brings to the house those unsuitable-looking bearded boyfriends. The third sister is Carol, the pig-tailed schoolgirl.

'It was simple enough to remember,' suggests Giles. 'A,B,C – Ann, Bridget and Carol. Some printer, at some stage, got the letters mixed up and reversed the names of Carol and Bridget. The confusion remained. Finally, Bridget became the youngest and Carol became the middle sister.'

The other mystery figure deserving of a brief examination is George Junior. It may seem to suggest, following a close study of the Family group, that George is the son of Vera and George the thinker (bookworm, philosopher, etc.). This, according to Giles – and he should know – is simply not the case. He insists that it has never been explained exactly where George Junior came from and that it is quite wrong to jump to conclusions. No one knows. Nor will they ever, apparently. However, the secret may lie in the fact that George Junior doubles as the celebrated note- and letter-writer, Giles Junior. It is Giles Junior who, when his cartooning creator is in hospital or laid up, writes a missive, amid ink blots and scruffy sketches, to the newspaper's readers.

His spelling is appalling and his punctuation non-existent. Nevertheless, he has, over the years, frequently come to the rescue when his father/creator/Svengali is indisposed.

"One of Grandma's light-weight, home-made loaves coming up."

Sunday Express, November 21st, 1965

Note George the bookworm, the Hampstead intellectual type – and Vera's husband – whose presence in the Family has always been a mystery. His is an entirely passive role in Family activities. His snivelling wife would have to shout at him in order to get him to his feet. But she never would. Theirs, surely, is a marriage made in Hades. Of all the partnerships in the Family it is the one that makes you shudder. Just imagine the quality of the pillow talk!

"Now we come to the bit where Father's come out without any money and Mother pays."

Sunday Express, March 13th, 1988

It is the size of the menu that is so depressing.

"It's the garage, Dad—the 'Happy Motorist Car Washer' you've bought Mum for Christmas is in."

Daily Express, December 19th, 1972

What is unsettling about Ernie, Father and Mother's youngest offspring, is the appearance he gives of being so unpleasantly mature – a little lad who combines the ordinary advantages of innocent childhood with sophisticated malice. There is no anxiety in him whatsoever. He is blessed with a malevolent tranquillity.

"I wasn't complaining about us being late getting it in the water—
I simply said the nights start drawing in again this month."

Sunday Express, June 2nd, 1985

Anyone who has prepared a boat for the sea will be particularly horrified by the appearance of a drill from within the hull – below the waterline.

"As we haven't had beef for so long I thought I'd be rash and treat ourselves to a piece of sirloin."

Sunday Express, May 12th, 1974

Butch would never get away with this in the real Giles home in Suffolk. Giles's wife Joan is far too practical. Butch wanders between the real and the cartoon world and, from the pet's point of view, there is always something to be said for a chaotic household where the occupants are distracted.

"We chained Grandma up to celebrate the Suffragettes anniversary and Butch has swallowed the key."

Sunday Express, July 2nd, 1978

Here, Ernie seems to have a quite remarkable knowledge of the early women's movement. Moreover, one cannot help considering the slightly indelicate question of whether or not Carol is wearing a bra. Giles took an almost prudish view of sexiness in his cartoons. He never drew voluptuous barmaids, for example.

"Mother, did you remember to tell the boys to save their bath water for the garden?"

Sunday Express, May 9th, 1976

The great drought of 1976. Britain bakes like the Sahara. Citizens are told to use their bath water on the flower beds.

At Lord's cricket ground, crowds cheered when rain stopped play for fifteen minutes. In Somerset, a vicar asked his congregation to give thanks to the Almighty for a brief downpour. To possess a dirty car was a demonstration of patriotism. Ice cream ran out. The clay bottoms of reservoirs were cracking in the heat.

And Grandma got drenched!

And thus it is that such analysis should cease. For as we come up against strange and inexplicable twists and turns in the behaviour patterns and in the Family tree itself, we must consider that we are dealing with another place here, a land where the rules are not always quite as our own. Much is best left undisturbed.

However, the more bizarre puzzles apart, there is a truth for us all to see. And recognise. After all, the Family has grown for some fifty years in the mind and heart of its perceptive creator. As occurs in real life, the characters have developed and become more complex, and their relationships have achieved depth, however disagreeable. Can there be, for example, a more suitable case for psychiatric examination than the friendship which exists between Grandma and Vera? It is a union which combines, from Grandma's point of view, an undoubted affection and sense of amusement with the most savage and sadistic cruelty. Vera, meanwhile, displays a slavish, unquestioning obedience and loyalty. Look about you, amongst the more complex and troubled relationships of your acquaintance, for an example of that. You won't have far to look.

It would seem appropriate at this point to repeat two startlingly contrasting views of the work of Giles and to apply them to the Family. The first is from the late ballerina, Dame Margot Fonteyn, a passionate admirer of the cartoonist whose signed photograph is one of the more precious among the many in the Giles sitting room in Suffolk.

Very few men can see clearly all the imperfections of face and form in the world around yet still retain an indulgent affection for humanity. Such a person is Giles. He must be a very compassionate man. Anyone else with his needle-sharp eyes would find it very hard not to be biting in their humour, but he mocks us only very gently. Even his most horrible characters are to some extent endearing. We laugh at them but also more often with them and sympathise with their plight. We can feel for all of them even when they are absolutely humourless and stupid. It always seems to me that my favourites are his children – those little no-necked monsters that reveal all the characteristics of the adults they will become, although it is noticeable that their faces are never completely stupid. They always show at least a natural intuition and vitality and there seems to be much more going on inside their busy little heads than in some of the self-satisfied grown-ups', spoiled perhaps by the influence of civilisation.

Great cartoonists fulfil a role similar to that of the ancient court jester, wrapping the truth in a clothing of humour to make it palatable. No one could criticise the monarch outright, but his jester could make a witticism that was both informative and acceptable. Giles does much the same thing. Let us all thank him for helping us to laugh at ourselves; it is the hardest lesson to learn and by far the most valuable.

This is the traditional view of Giles. There were those who saw less of the whimsical angel and more of the demon.

That great *Daily Express* commentator, Nathaniel Gubbins, wrote:

From Dean Swift to Giles the men who have made you laugh most have been savage men. Thoughtless people have lumped them together under the title humorist, which would include knockabout comedians and clowns. But the laughter-makers who have been remembered, and who will be remembered in the years to come, are the satirists – the men who hate. Among the things they hate are stupidity, injustice, intolerance. If they have suffered from any of these, or all, so much the better for their art. This hatred, combined with a possible subconscious desire for perfection in an imperfect world, produced men like Giles. I don't know what it is that Giles hates most. Maybe it's ugly and wicked children. Maybe it's hunting squires and hard-riding women. Maybe it's ancient aunts in hideous hats who always arrive for Christmas, or whenever there's a picnic or a free holiday. Whichever it is, cartoonist Giles has had his revenge on them all.

Whatever the truth, there is little point in asking Giles himself to comment on these contrasting views of his artistry. It is fruitless to interrogate artists about the whys and wherefores of their creations, for usually they are unable to enlighten you – or themselves – to any great degree. However, in the case of Carl Giles it is agreeably easy to see and rewarding to discover just how many of the richly endowed and very real characters that people Gilesland spring from the life and robust experiences of their inspired creator.

Grandma

Grandma would sell her soul to the Devil, if she had not already done so, for a winner on the 2.30 at Towcester races. If she knew the whereabouts of a stash of forged £50 notes she would dig it up at midnight and be at the local sales – or at the bookies, more likely – first thing in the morning.

Grandma would certainly rob a bank if she could get away with it, and would doubtless have acted as lookout, had she been invited, for the Great Train Robbers. She once even kidnapped the Chancellor of the Exchequer.

She is chillingly and malevolently ruthless, too. Should a suspicious missive arrive during a letter-bomb scare, she would settle herself behind a pile of sandbags, put a helmet on and send frail, snuffling Vera off to some distant point in order to open it. This is not a fiction. She did that very thing. Vera survived.

Vera, within the Family, is Grandma's chum and apparent confidante. However, one of the few things in life

which will bring a broad un-Christian grin to the old bat's features is Vera's discomfort and misery.

All these disagreeable considerations aside, it is Grandma's physical energies and endless youthful skills which make her particularly formidable. She is a confident horsewoman, a pole vaulter of Olympic pretentions, rides a motor-cycle with the ferocity of a Hell's Angel, sails a boat like Uffa Fox, can probably drive a tank, almost certainly fight a bull and definitely toss the caber at least as far as the hairiest Highlander.

She plays the bagpipes, too.

The old girl quenches the raging thirst aroused by such vigorous activity with a quantity of Guinness which would stun a bar full of Irish brickies.

Grandma is also a patriot, a Royalist, at times a good socialist and frequently the scourge of petty bureaucracy. She will show her ability to act with extreme violence, knocking huge men off their feet with a weighty handbag when aroused over such matters as parking fines or the poll tax.

Together with all of this

"I broke all me Noo Year resolutions first day. Done yours yet, sir?"

Daily Express, Jan. 4th, 1947

It is not generally known that Giles created two Grandmas. The first was a prototype, but was joined by a second. They were, for a while, competing figures within the one granny, like Jekyll and Hyde. In the early days the nice, cheeky, happy granny, antithesis of the frightening, ogreish version, would make an occasional appearance. Here she is in one of Giles's more delightful early cartoons.

"Watch 'im Vera—he'll have your heart out and shove it in Mrs. Harris before you can say Happy New Year."

Daily Express, Jan. 4th, 1968

Here is the other gran, the Grandma that we all know and fear. The only time she smiles – almost – is when she is sending her Family companion, the snuffling, ridiculous Vera, off to some torment or other.

This drawing touches on one of the more remarkable medical achievements of the century. A month earlier in South Africa, a team of surgeons led by Dr Christiaan Barnard had carried out the first successful human heart transplant at Groote Schuur Hospital, Cape Town. Those of us with a sense of compassion must wonder how Vera's heart would have fared had this unhappy organ been used as a transplant.

"Thank you so much for calling and advising me on the changes I must make in 1987. Now hop it."

Daily Express, December 30th, 1986

Giles drew a very flattering picture of Maggie Thatcher. It was said that those men who most despised Maggie often found her unsettlingly alluring. Not Giles, surely.

"You didn't plough any fields and scatter—you nicked that marrow from my allotment on the way here."

Sunday Express, October 2nd, 1966

It is always encouraging to know that Grandma went to church. She had much to confess, after all. Still, apart from this particular lady's sins and her pressing need for redemption, there is much detail in this cartoon which, as usual, is wonderfully rewarding. The funniest thing for this reader is the fact that George the bookworm is not singing from his hymn book, but simply reading it. George would not understand the principle of converting the written word into song. He would regard those ignorant people caterwauling about him as completely barmy.

Here she is in all her magnificence – the real Grandma Giles. The funny thing is that Giles himself says he based his fictional Grandma on his actual grandmothers. The woman we see here, however, is proud, upright and Victorian in all the best senses of the word. Giles was in awe of her. He recalls that she was stern, though warm and loving. It was only when arthritis confined her to a wheelchair that the young Giles took advantage of her. He would wheel her around her square near London's King's Cross at a speed that caused her knuckles to grow white and her hair to ruffle in the slip-stream.

She bore it, admits her grandson, with the fortitude that is a mark of her breed and never seemed to hold it against him.

44

the black-garbed, ferocious Giles matriarch – English suburban *passionara* – is a domestic soul, often seen sitting with a newspaper, or snoozing, with Butch the dog at her feet, snug by the fire. She is God-fearing, too. Why, she even goes to church.

So, it is a puzzle what to make of her. But whatever she might appear to be under close scrutiny, she is certainly one of the most celebrated and – quite extraordinarily – most adored grandmothers in the history of grandmothers.

She represents anarchy, of course. And she is thus identified with the young. Indeed, there is something in Grandma for all of us. But it is the old rebel, the feisty, stout battler with not a shred of pretentiousness, that we all love. There is no humbug in Grandma. Or not much!

So where did she come from? It is true to say that she arrived slowly. She crept up on us. She evolved.

Giles acknowledges that his prototype Grandma made her first appearance some years before August 1945, while he was drawing cartoons for *Reynolds News*. She was first seen mischievously standing between a couple of tommies. She is an altogether jollier creature, certainly nothing like the Grandma of later times. The only recognisable features are the floral hat, black coat and handbag. And the mischief, maybe.

As the years passed the smiling face was slowly to collapse until it was merely a straight mouth under large circular specs, crunched down into a scarcely visible, truculent chin by a hat, not placed gently on the head, but yanked into position with a single act of great force. The jolly, thriving bunch of flowers of the original soon flattened out, and eventually a small cloth bird made its appearance alongside the flora. This creature attracted much attention from the beasts of the air and was particularly popular with gulls at the seaside.

Grandma lost the white pinny on her front, and the white handbag of the earlier version became black and grew in size. Eventually it was to be given the protection of a padlock and a spare chain for attaching to the sturdy legs of tavern tables. Grandma's feet were to disappear and were only seen, thereafter, on the odd occasion when she was observed upside down in a ditch or falling out of a sailing dinghy.

A fox stole was also added to Grandma's outfit. But that disappeared soon after the protests of animal lovers made themselves heard in Gilesland. The old girl was happy to take on a dozen enemies at once, but not a howling mob. She was, after all, a pragmatic soul.

What, people frequently ask, was the inspiration for this awesome creation? Did Giles ever know such a person? It is not likely. However, Giles claims that there is a bit of both of his own grandmothers in Grandma.

The real Grandma Giles was a handsome, straight-backed, typically Victorian matriarch with a bustle at her posterior and white lace about her wrists. She was a lady, so typical of that time, with poise and elegance and strength of character and with the mix of authority and kindness that commands respect and discipline and, occasionally, fear. It is a long-extinct breed.

'You behaved yourself,' says Giles. 'You wouldn't even think of trying anything on.

'Grandma Giles was a churchgoing lady and didn't drink, although she would have the odd brandy and Guinness for medicinal purposes. She was very strict but compassionate. She had a lovely gentle, slight smile. And she was always Grandma Giles. You would never, never call her Granny. You respected her and you certainly never took a chance with her.'

That is not entirely true. When Grandma Giles grew older and less formidable and was confined to a wheelchair with rheumatoid arthritis, young Giles and the odd mischievous cousin did take fearful advantage of the lady.

"Grandma, it's not fair to send Vera all that way on her own to open your letters."

Daily Express, September 22nd, 1972

These were the days of a particularly cowardly form of terrorism: the letter bomb. And here is Grandma at her very worst. She enjoys tormenting her close Family chum Vera, but this is taking things to the limit.

Here is Grandma terrorising Vera again. Experts in firearms will notice that she is holding a Luger automatic pistol, the sidearm used by Wehrmacht officers in World War Two.

The occasion was the General Election of 1970. The day after Grandma's polling activities, the Tories were voted back into power with Edward Heath as their leader. Grandma must have been Tory by nature, though she often seemed to express socialist views. Her politics were confusing, like those of her creator, Giles. He drove a Bentley, lived like a king, but was once a communist.

"They'll get hey nonny nonny if one of 'em lands on Grandma's foot."

Sunday Express, May 3rd, 1987

Anyone who finds the pastoral English diversion of morris dancing both preposterous and inexplicable will sympathise with the sentiments expressed here.

"Dad—is there any rule that we have to pay Grandma Capital Gains Tax on her winnings?"

Sunday Express, April 11th, 1965

Grandma is addicted to gambling. And apart from her peculiar relationship with Vera, she seems to relate only to children.

Nanny Clarke, Giles's other grandmother. It is difficult to see, once again, how this gentle, cosy woman could possibly have been even part-model for the cartoon Grandma. Nanny Clarke lived in Norfolk and ran a jolly household. She was always cooking pastries and puffing up pillows and, just occasionally, bringing out the whisky to celebrate something or other.

Giles insists that we should look beyond the obvious in his cartoon Grandma. 'She has a lot of warmth and a great sense of humour,' he says.

Grandma Giles, whose husband Alfred, the former jockey to Edward VII, had died at the age of fifty-three, lived with two spinster daughters in Myddelton Square, not far from Islington. All the family dwelt within walking distance.

Giles was required to push his grandmother, on occasion, from one address to the other. This he did with great speed, occasionally and unnecessarily making more than one circuit of the square. He would, he recalls with some merriment, propel the conveyance as fast as his legs would allow.

The spokes of the invalid chair blurred and the little lad's legs pumped like frenzied pistons, the slip-stream stirring the neat grey curls at the lady's temples, her knuckles slowly draining of blood as she gripped the arms.

'She never complained,' said Giles. 'She was tough, one of a breed. She was proud and was not going to show any weakness to us little devils.'

The other grandmother, Nanny Clarke, lived up in Norfolk. Her neat house on the outskirts of Norwich offered a second home to the young Giles and it was an altogether more welcoming, informal haven. Nanny Clarke was a much cosier figure, with soft features, gentle hands, white wavy hair, a ready smile and an uninhibited welcome.

She was the sort of lady who usually had traces of flour on her hands and a dusting of it on her nose where she had wiped away a tear from the peeling of onions. She was a grandmother who was always making beds and cooking pies and puffing up cushions and mending small holes and washing dishes and winding endless family garments, sodden from the great aluminium laundry bin, through the mangle.

'The house was always full of laughing, happy people,' recalls Giles. 'No one wanted for anything.'

They weren't very well off when things went badly for them, but Nanny Clarke would always come back from the shops with food and toys and a bottle of whisky for visitors. She enjoyed a social drink, too.

She liked the excuse – enjoyed the sense of occasion – when friends came to call.

It is difficult to see very much of these two ladies in the frightening figure created by their grandson. He seems to have been a Dr Frankenstein who brought to life a monster which soon got out of hand and in which, even when it was too late, he insisted that he saw goodness.

'There is a lot of warmth in Grandma,' says Giles.

That may very well be. But her creator, like Frankenstein, finally wanted to kill her off. He had expressed his intention to do so quite a few years ago. And while he had not actually devised a plan for her destruction, the very thought of such a thing is quite appalling. What would he have done? There could be few suitable ways for such a figure to meet her Maker, though there was the time that she was nearly felled, tumbling and cartwheeling, by horses competing in the Grand National after she had scampered across windswept Aintree to collect her betting slip.

Lost at sea? Just her flower-decorated hat, a seagull investigating the cloth bird, found by the sea shore? Whatever, Giles was determined to do her in. The aftermath, it must be said, would have provided endless fun for the artist. Imagine the scenes in the funeral parlour and think what would have happened on the day of Grandma's interment. (She wouldn't have been cremated. Cremations do not take place in Gilesland.)

There would surely have been a period of lying in state, during which relatives were required to pay their last respects. But just consider what irreverent disruption there would have been under the bed, just outside the door, beneath the coffin, even.

As for the funeral itself, one can only speculate. Perhaps the old girl would have been floated down the Thames, like her great hero, Winston Churchill, on a magnificent barge. Shipyard cranes would have bowed in respect. Solemn, muffled drums would have sounded. The Queen would have worn black and a veil. Who knows? It would certainly have been one of those strange days in life when fiction would have joined hands with reality. We would all have mourned Grandma as if she had been real. Well, she was, in a way. Still is.

"Watch 'im Vera."

Daily Express, November 25th, 1982

Giles based Vera on certain women from his childhood who smelt, he recalls, of doctors' surgeries and out-patients' departments. Passing one on the street, you caught a whiff of camphorated oil, a medicament with an aromatic smell and a bitter taste, used in pharmacy and as an insect repellent.

Here Grandma smiles again. It is unclear whether her remark is an instruction or a warning.

52

"Stand by for some real fireworks—Grandma's just found what's left of her hat you used on the guy."

Sunday Express, November 6th, 1988

The hut in the Family's garden, which seems forever to change its shape, position and purpose, is a most curious place. Here, the Family friend Stinker, with help from Ernie, is attending to a whole shelf of hedgehogs.

"Pity. Vera's thrived on it all her life."

Daily Express, November 27th, 1969

The implications of significant international events, such as US President Nixon's policy on germ warfare, are often reduced to the most simple domestic level in the Giles Family household. Vera's coughs and sneezes spray out bugs like one of those aerosol cans of insecticide.

Grandma has a smile on her face here. Close followers of Grandma will confirm that this phenomenon almost always occurs when Vera is in discomfort.

"Never mind who I'm voting for—which of them let you in here?"

Sunday Express, June 7th, 1987

The wonderful Stinker, mute observer of all that occurs in the Giles Family household, takes a picture of Grandma in the bath. He is always there to catch the action where others fear to go. In later years he became cartoonist Giles's favourite character. Stinker and Grandma are the real stars of the show.

"She says she hasn't missed the opening of the Flat since she was eight."

Daily Express, March 26th, 1987

They say it is the sport of kings. For those of us who do not favour this disreputable activity, Grandma's punting pursuits are, without doubt, the most unattractive of her obsessions.

"Off you go and rejoice—and steer clear of the Falklands 200 mile restricted zone."

Daily Express, May 2nd, 1982

The Falklands War was at its height. Giles is making merry with the 200-mile restriction zone around the Islands.

It was on the day that this sketch was published, however, that the Argentinian cruiser, the General Belgrano, *was sunk, with the loss of hundreds of lives.*

This cartoon, by the evening, had taken on a somewhat grim significance. Giles disagreed with the Falklands adventure.

Somehow, the plan for her end was leaked and it reached the ears of the old girl's admirers, many of them her allies, the young. There was an outcry. Grandma was reprieved. She lived on to terrorise Gilesland with renewed vigour.

There was another surprise concerning Grandma. We were to learn that she wasn't the only Giles Grandma. During a Family visit to Manchester we saw her being greeted by her two Mancunian sisters. They looked identical and had emerged, to the astonishment and delight of *Express* readers, scuttling in joyous greeting out of one of the city's side streets. Why had we never heard about them before?

It was almost as if they were proliferating in some terrifying way. Would there be a Scottish Grandma? A Welsh Grandma? 'No, but there was an Irish one,' says Giles. 'And could she drink. She turned up after one of our visits to Ireland. She was very like the South of England Grandma. She looked exactly like her and, in fact, like the Manchester sisters – but in terms of Guinness she could probably drink them all under the table.'

Who was the original Grandma, then? Whence, in terms of the rich store of material in her creator's head, had she hailed? Many believed that she was based on Lord Beaverbrook, the great newspaper proprietor and Giles's employer. But a few had a different theory, one which makes rather more sense and which is certainly shared by the author of this book. Grandma is Giles himself.

'I have no doubt at all,' says the artist's friend, Johnny Speight, creator of his own monster in the shape of Cockney bigot Alf Garnett. 'Giles is there in Grandma, all the way through. She has his spirit and his mischief. She's the scourge of everything which Giles hates, after all – everything from VAT inspectors to traffic wardens get walloped. Of course he's Grandma.'

It is worth examining the notion. And it is even worth suggesting, indeed, that Giles, in some respects, actually looks a little like Grandma. He has short white hair, glasses and – as often as not – displays a set of the mouth which can alter from impious merriment to ferocious disapproval within seconds.

Giles is incensed by the use and abuse of power by minor, pompous figures of authority and thus hates everyone from gas inspectors to traffic wardens – especially traffic wardens – and from flower-show officials to railway-crossing keepers. Giles has never, unlike Grandma, taken openly to physical violence. Ever since his schooldays when he sought the protection of tougher boys he has shied away from the thud and whack of fist in face and bone on bone. But he may well enjoy the satisfaction of such well-placed aggression through the good offices of this stout-hearted and fearless, black-garbed, handbag-thrashing defender of his frequently outraged principles. Whack. There is tremendous force in the full impact of one of the lady's better-aimed blows. Huge men are lifted off their feet.

Giles hates travelling salesmen and regards anyone who comes uninvited to the door, be it a prospective member of Parliament or a pimply-faced boy selling dusters and oven cleaner, as a vile intruder.

Sitting in his wheelchair in more recent times he would dispatch them with a curse. Grandma would clout them with the handbag, a deep-pocketed leather satchel which some believe to contain knobs of church roofing lead.

Giles has been a horseman, a yachtsman of note and a motor-cyclist. All of these activities are shared by Grandma. Giles likes the races. As does Grandma.

However, most significantly, Grandma – despite all her anarchy and deplorable behaviour – represents a toughness and determination, a British stubbornness and indefatigability, which is also shared by the man who created her.

It would thus seem appropriate to bring up to date the situation, at the time of writing, concerning Carl Giles's health. In *Giles: A Life in Cartoons* I wrote of

58

"Stand by for a fab bout of Blackpool hospitality, daddyo—here come two of Grandma's northern sisters."

Daily Express, December 2nd, 1963

The notion is too dreadful to contemplate. But it has to be faced. There is more than one Grandma. Here, the old girl is being joyously greeted by her two North Country sisters. They are identical. The Family are gathered about the caravan which, in reality, was a mobile studio. Giles toured the country with it, taking his characters with him.

Their associated adventures are chronicled in the following chapter.

"For this one I want time and a half, danger money and a month in the Bahamas after each visit."

Daily Express, July 22nd, 1977

Giving Grandma an intimate examination with a stethoscope is one responsibility for which no remuneration would be adequate.

the sorry circumstances of Giles who, within a period of twelve months and at the age of seventy-six, had had both his legs amputated beneath the knee. Most men of his age, suffering such appalling medical misfortune, would have thrown in the rag and given up.

Giles has fought with the spirit of the war ace Sir Douglas Bader, and is now able to wear a new pair of legs and has regained some mobility.

"I know she's not likely to carry many £50 notes—but with her we check the pounds."

Daily Express, April 24th, 1984

It goes without saying that in the world of commerce, Grandma is treated as a serious hazard.

During the course of Giles's therapy there was much cursing. There was at times what might have appeared to some observers to have been a harsh disregard for the sensibilities of those who urged caution and rest. All of this, of course, was very much in the spirit of Grandma.

However, it should be said that there are those who find the combative, awkward, cussed, sometimes thoughtless and bloody-minded behaviour shared by Carl Giles and his most celebrated fictional character less than a cause for amusement. Many have been brought to their knees in despair.

"Mr Billy Graham has told America that one in four first-born Britons are born out of wedlock, so Grandma insists that we find her birth certificate."

Daily Express, Mar. 18th, 1954

Once again, Grandma's age comes up for consideration. We are also required to imagine her as a babe, mewling and puking – presumably – in her nurse's arms. It is a shocking thought.

"Playing up 'ell because she couldn't find her woolly egg warmer on show."

Daily Express, August 6th, 1981

Grandma was a fanatical Royalist. However, it is difficult to sympathise with her point of view on this occasion. Can there be anything more outrageous than having to pay money to view the Aladdin's cave of booty which Prince Charles and Princess Diana accrued at the time of their wedding?

"Grandma! For heaven's sake forget there's a grandma competing in the Olympic Games—you're too late for the selectors, anyway."

Daily Express, August 18th, 1960

Grandma, an Olympic pole vaulter? Why not? Incidentally, it is easy to miss the fact that cameraman Stinker is perched in the most magnificent position to capture the action. Any Fleet Street sports desk would have been proud of him.

"That was a bright stroke telling Grandma there is a famous Grandma-artist in America who is 100 years old and didn't take up painting till she was 77."

Daily Express, September 6th, 1960

Giles at his most inspired.

"Next year we'll order a slap-up meal after we know the result of the last race."

Daily Express, June 22nd, 1962

For many years Grandma wore a fox fur around her neck. Imagine how that would go down in the Royal Enclosure during these enlightened times.

"Now the war is over I assume you have decided to risk the perils of travel and give us a look."

Sunday Express, March 3rd, 1991

To suggest that Grandma is a coward is notably un-Christian and woefully inaccurate. She may be many things, but she is not one to scuttle for the broom cupboard when the flak is flying. Although it has to be said that she would almost certainly push Vera over the top first in order to judge the direction of the bullets.

"If he once mentions Olympic Games or tells us we're all runners in the great race against evil, I'm withdrawing to the Spotted Cow."

Sunday Express, August 5th, 1984

We can certainly sympathise with this fear of Grandma's. There are times, indeed, when it is easy to warm to the old bat.

"Here she comes—will we take back 200 tins of Argentine corned beef she's been hoarding since Suez?"

Daily Express, April 8th, 1982

The patriot!

A man who has had his share of trouble, poor fellow, was the sculptor commissioned to create a bronze work for the centre of Ipswich, a fiftieth anniversary tribute to the artist in his home town. Miles Robinson was honoured, though he could not have been prepared for what was to follow.

The sculpture depicts Grandma, the snuffling Vera, the robust young twins and, lying across the front at the old girl's feet, Butch the dog.

Giles had been invited to view and comment on the statue before it was committed irretrievably to bronze, prompting him to make an extraordinary,

69

almost unheard-of public outing. The television cameras, devices regarded with a deep loathing by Giles, had approached and poked their lenses towards the cartoonist's face as he squinted uncertainly at the half-ton work of art before him. Giles had snarled and growled at the intrusive contraptions and refused to respond to reporters' questions. Miles Robinson could hardly have been encouraged.

Approval of a sort was given and the group of characters was finally cast in bronze. Giles spotted the finished article in a colour photograph in his local newspaper and exploded with rage. 'This is nothing like Butch at all,' he stormed to his long-suffering wife Joan. Grimacing at the journal on his lap, he declared, 'I want it out. I want it off the statue. What's his number?'

It should be explained here that Butch was both real and fictional, one of those many aspects of Gilesland where truth and invention come together, cross-fertilised. There had always been a real Butch, or rather, a long succession of dogs named Butch, culminating in the Airedale who slept in the Giles home for much of the time by the fire or in the sun by the French windows. But then the same Butch also featured in the cartoons, usually with Grandma. Whether Giles was expressing outrage at

Sculptor Miles Robinson with his bronze of Grandma and Butch. (East Anglian Daily Times)

"Mrs Thatcher would certainly give Grandma's State Benefits a radical overhaul if she knew they all went on Lester Piggott yesterday."

Daily Express, June 6th, 1985

Giles worked the most astonishing magic with the Family's back garden. Here, it looks enormous. There is certainly no feeling of a poky corner of suburbia. It almost has the feeling of a stately home.

the misrepresentation of the real Butch or the fictional Butch was not clear.

In any case, the appalled Robinson was then instructed, mercilessly, to remove Butch entirely from the finished sculpture. It wasn't possible, of course, without starting the whole thing over again – practically from the first fistful of clay.

Those who had witnessed all this persuaded Giles to

71

relent. Which he did. Just. He reluctantly called Robinson and said: 'The feeling seems to be that you had better leave Butch in. But I still think it's bloody awful.'

The statue, with Butch, survived. And it will doubtless be standing, collecting the usual pigeon droppings, in hundreds of years' time. 'Meet you by Grandma,' the youth of that future Ipswich will no doubt be saying. She'll live on. And so will Giles. Difficult so-and-sos both. But how we have loved them.

There are moments when you really warm to Grandma. Poker with Santa at five past two on Christmas morning – and winning his pocket watch – shows incomparable style.

Giles's love of toy soldiers and forts bring this old annual cover to glorious life.

What a magnificently drawn elephant. Giles became close friends with the artists of Bertram Mills Circus. His animal drawings always brought a startling touch of photographic reality to cartoons where the human figures, while recognisable, were caricatures.

Don't those hunting types look odious?

It is not often that a joke is simple in a Giles drawing. This is simplicity itself. There are no other subplots unfolding, nothing to distract the eye except the pleasing nature of a sunny glade. No furry creature stirs, no evil child is evident.
Often Giles's central joke is the less impressive aspect of his work. Not here.

Steamrollers and trams, mechanical creations to bring a symphony to the heart of Giles.

How far will the little monsters go?

Stinker, with his Pentax, beautifully positioned again for a study in catastrophe.

There was no cartoonist's brush which could so effectively and powerfully fill a sail as Giles's did.

It has nothing to do with railway trains, but here Giles manages to slip in a heartfelt plug for his most favoured of charities, the Royal National Lifeboat Institution.

What a satisfying act of vandalism this is!

CHAPTER THREE

The Giles Family on Holiday

In one respect Giles was like old Toad of Toad Hall. He wasn't a boastful fellow and he certainly wasn't fat and puffed up, but he loved big gleaming motor cars and boats. He would drive around at enormous speed in his beloved white roadster, the Jaguar XJ 120, with a helmet and goggles on and a look of malevolent pleasure on his face. In Toad-like manner he hated petty authority that contrived to frustrate his motoring. He raged both at railway-crossing gatekeepers – on one occasion he shouted at a keeper's darkened cottage window in the early hours until the man finally appeared, still in his pyjamas – and traffic wardens. Here, indeed, Giles might be seen as a mixture of Toad and Grandma, the road-hogging speed merchant combined with the black-garbed, brolly-wielding matriarchal scourge of absurdly self-important, bureaucratic little people who tyrannically boss and inconvenience free-spirited citizens of the highway.

Giles derived equal pleasure from being at the helm of his magnificent sailing yacht and was, for many years, a familiar and popular character about the estuary. He would turn up in waterside taverns and always cause a stir; inevitably chat up the barmaid and buy drinks for the usual gathering of ruddy-faced mariners in navy blue polo-necked sweaters and squeaky yellow foul-weather gear.

However, it was Giles's caravan which was the most remarkable love of his travelling life. It was a device that linked his fictional cartoon world, and in particular the Family, with the very real existence of Carl Giles the artist, lover of wheels, traveller and master of DIY. This extraordinary home-built caravan-cum-studio, towed for thousands of miles by the cartoonist in his early Landrover, toured the British Isles and established, as it went, an immediate reputation as a kind of ever-open, free-to-all-comers, voyaging public house. Huge consignments of alcoholic beverages were taken on board every time the caravan slowed to walking pace.

It should be recalled here that Giles loved a drink. Just as Grandma did, of course, although it is rare, when the cartoon adventures are examined, to see any of the Family the worse for wear. While they are sometimes seen in a tavern with a glass in attendance they are never, as are the lurching, guffawing neighbours who crash in on Christmas Eve wearing paper hats, tipsy. Grandma, despite lashing back pints of Guinness, always has her wits about her. One feels, almost, as if there would be quite a lot of disapproval from certain quarters of the Family if any one of them became unduly fixed to the bottle – despite the pub-dwelling reputation of their creator. There is little evidence of an overdeveloped sense of propriety amongst the Family, and they have coped well with such difficulties as Grandma's criminal tendencies, the psychopathic behaviour of the younger children and

Giles, a carpenter's pencil tucked in professionally over his ear, drills a precision-measured hole in the framework of his caravan. His DIY abilities astonished everyone. The caravan itself was constructed like a vintage aircraft, the wooden frame being covered with light metal sheeting.

It was wonderfully well appointed and offered first-class luxury, not only to Mr and Mrs Giles, but for all the many visitors along the route who were entertained with the traditionally plentiful, usually liquid, Giles hospitality.

The completed caravan shows the studio section, with its own windscreen wiper, lowered and ready. The compartment simply rotated outwards and downwards with the aid of a well-oiled mechanism – and in moments became a studio ready for the mobile draughtsman to use.

the never-mentioned wartime GI fatherhood of the twins; yet they seem to regard intoxication as a weakness which is beyond the pale. It has to be said that Grandma was once apprehended by the police in the days before the breathalyser, and was required to walk along a straight yellow kerbside line without faltering to left or right. She seemed to pass the test to the law's satisfaction, though they would quite obviously have loved to have nicked the old menace and clapped her in irons.

Still, as far as the caravan was concerned, it was a jolly home to them all. As recorded by the cartoons in the *Daily* and *Sunday Express* it was the nomadic quarters of not only the artist and his wife, but all of his best-loved creations: Father, Mother, the twins, and, of course, Grandma.

The Giles family left this morning (weather permitting or not) by caravan for its holiday.

Daily Express, Aug. 14th, 1951

Giles had built himself a caravan, an extraordinary vehicle which was both luxury home and travelling studio. His employers in London had viewed the project from afar as simply one of those eccentricities which they had come to expect of the unpredictable cartoonist. They were not then to know what a role it would play in the years to come.

The original caravan – there was a successor, which incorporated design improvements – had been constructed amidst the outbuildings of Giles's Suffolk farm. It was to become the travelling home, both of the cartoonist and Joan, and – in a surreal sense – the Family members. Fact and fiction merged to produce wonderful material for the Daily Express.

Here, the Family sets out in exaggeratedly inclement August weather to tour the Kingdom.

"Right. You've convinced me you can walk a straight line for a mile—now come back to the station while I charge you."

Daily Express, December 21st, 1962

This was before the breathalyser. Grandma could hold her drink like a Cossack. She could have walked a white line the length of the country and back, and never lost her balance. She probably could have done it on a tightrope.

The caravan was constructed over a year amidst the outbuildings at the Giles's Suffolk farm. It was an extraordinary, eccentric piece of DIYing, and seemed to borrow as much from aircraft design as from caravan-making. The wooden ribbing which formed its frame might well have been the basic structure for the fuselage of an early World War Two bomber, and the notion was confirmed later when Giles added what looked like an aeroplane fin.

It was, in fact, a gravity-feed tank for the caravan's water supply of fifty gallons, built to aerodynamic specifications. From the provisions of this fin the Gileses – and presumably the Family – washed, showered, rinsed the dishes and filled the kettle.

However, the strangest aspect of this huge travelling home was that one end could be adapted to form a studio for its artist owner. A section in the side was unlocked when required and simply rotated outwards and downwards to form a brightly lit area which included a sloped drawing board, shelves, pigeonholes and any other of the gimmicks and gadgetry required to produce cartoons. The window of this studio even had its own windscreen wiper.

For the benefit of Joan, ever the superb hostess, there was a luxuriously equipped galley whose glittering and gleaming mod cons would have certainly been the envy of a Mrs Toad, should such a person ever have existed. The interior was beautifully finished, everything shiny and polished, and the bed was comfortable enough for an emperor and empress.

The lighting was complex and the night-time atmosphere could be adjusted from bright and garish to subtle and cosy. The final electrical flourish, a touch of Giles's high-tech ingenuity on the back exterior of the vehicle, was particularly interesting in that it betrayed the intolerance which Giles himself had previously held towards caravans owned by other people. When blocked by one of these swaying holiday homes on wheels, especially when driving his Jag XJ 120, he would curse like Toad and lean to the

right in a permanently frustrated attempt to see if the road ahead was clear. He admits to honking his horn with unseemly fury.

Giles was determined not to be regarded as a similar menace. The Giles caravan had two very big indicator arrows and a large sign which lit up when the road ahead was clear and informed those behind: 'Ready to be overtaken'. Motorists, reported the artist, waved merrily as they sped past.

They were unaware, needless to say, that they were passing the mobile home of Britain's greatest cartoonist and his celebrated clan of creations.

And thus it was that for several seasons in the early fifties the Giles caravan, drawn by a sturdy old Landrover, with Giles at the wheel and loyal Joan by his side, set off about the country. At each stop, the door flew wide, the bar flew open, the studio was lowered with the gentle hiss of well-oiled machinery and, magically, Grandma and her tribe spilled out to mix – on sketching paper, at any rate – with natives, from Cornwall to the Highlands, from Sunningdale to John o'Groats. It was during the Giles circus's travels north of the border that the artist offered his readers the proof that cartoon and reality had joined forces. In a Disney-style picture he featured a photograph of his caravan, surrounded by a sketch of Family members. It is here that we see Grandma playing the bagpipes, Father and Mother in tartan and George the bookworm with his ever-unlit pipe and with his nose in a copy of Robbie Burns's poetry.

Giles enjoyed his tours of Scotland and he particularly favoured Scottish hospitality. Such was the abundant nature of the mutual entertaining which occurred on both the High Road and the Low Road that Giles was moved to print the following disclaimer

(OPPOSITE) *Here is Giles, with his protractors, paints, Anglepoise lamp and ashtray all conveniently positioned, at work on a cartoon.*

"What have we stopped to celebrate this time—the Battle of Bannockburn or Battle of Britain Week?"

Daily Express, Sept. 15th, 1954

Giles loved Scotland. So did the Family. There were several trips over the years and there was scarcely a *Highland tavern which was not visited. Note the wonderfully detailed north-of-the-border stonework.*

"I see you're taking the Loch Ness Monster back with you."

Daily Express, Sept. 18th, 1954

Can that be Stinker, up on the tower, fishing?

in the *Daily Express:* 'Should there be any minor discrepancies in tartans, accents or other details which may offend the Highlander, Giles asks that it may be taken into consideration that apart from the 1954 weather and the effort of hauling thirty-six feet of studio up and down mountains he had also to contend with some pretty stiff bouts of Scottish hospitality.'

Giles adored Scotland. But it was to the Highland Games that Giles and his Family were particularly drawn. There were a number of cartoons dispatched

from this celebrated Royal Braemar event, and the opportunities for the Family to get stuck into the various sporting activities were rich with comic possibility.

With that other family, the Royals, always fully turned out at Braemar, Giles was also fulfilling his unofficial role as unpaid court jester, sending up a Scottish sporting event which the American tourist sees as quaint, and the average Sassenach as barking mad and primitive.

"Well—we've seen Balmoral from the air, stalked our first deer . . . now what do we do?"

Daily Express, Sept. 10th, 1954

Grandma at bay!

"Look out, Dad! Here comes the man to say no more Highland Games rehearsals."

Sunday Express, Sept. 5th, 1954

The two arrows on the back of the caravan are an example of the thoughtful nature of Giles's technology. He was well aware of the irritation that these road-hogging mobile homes caused to other travellers and was determined to make his own caravan as highway-friendly as possible.

A later development was an illuminated sign which advised motorists behind that it was safe to overtake.

Interestingly, he never actually featured members of the Royal family at Braemar in his cartoons. 'That was deliberate,' says Giles, who regarded the Games as a private function. However, he was frequently asked by them for originals of those cartoons he drew on other occasions in which they did appear.

"Sh! Here comes the Dickie Bird."

Daily Express, Sept. 11th, 1954

There are few artists who can make height look quite so frightening. Focus, if you dare, on the caravan.

"Goodbye, and don't forget—next holiday you bring the Coronation Stone and we'll get you a couple of salmon."

Daily Express, Sept. 15th, 1954

Farewell to Scotland!

Disaster was to strike in Derbyshire. Giles had mis-calculated the stress and strength factors of the wheels. There was a horrible crunching and grinding and the caravan simply slumped on its axle. The weather was typical Giles weather. He can be seen in this picture, with Joan, shielding his ever-present fag from the rain.

They had to wait twenty-four hours before replacement wheels were delivered.

There were times when you drew and times when you didn't. If I had included them in those Braemar events it would have been like I was being overfamiliar in a way – like some comedians tend to be. I would have hated for them to think that I was out of line. And it would have been out of line, somehow. The photographers were always poking their lenses at them there. I didn't want to be seen to be doing the same thing with my drawings.

Royals apart, the caravan was always of great interest at these events.

People were attracted to it – either because it was so unusual or because they recognised it, I suppose, as the caravan in the cartoons. We would have all kinds of huge Scotsmen in kilts coming in for a drink. They were massive, hairy and muscular figures and their hands were so big that you didn't see the glass they were holding, you just saw them lift what appeared to be their closed fist to their mouth. And – bang – down would go another dram. We had to be pretty well stocked up with whisky. But we were useful for other reasons. Once when the Games were drenched with a downpour the drummers came in with these drumsticks with big woollen balls at the end for Joan to dry out over the stove. You can imagine the sound effect and the horrible splash when hitting a drum with one of those sodden things. Joan just rotated them over the heat until each of the ends of the sticks went from being a soggy fluffy mess to a dry, firm ball again. You could hear the difference when the band struck up.

These caravan trips were an enormous success. They continued over the years and into the sixties. But they were not without their setbacks and minor hitches. The maiden voyage, for example, saw its own brief catastrophe. Giles and Joan had set off merrily from their farmhouse at Ipswich. It was a bit like the launch of a ship.

Here, finally, was this magnificent structure which had grown slowly but with a splendid sense of confidence and destiny in a gap between the cluster of buildings on the Giles's estate.

Hundreds and hundreds of man-hours – mostly Giles's – had gone into its creation. Now, here it was, with two coats of paint, curtains in the windows, electrics working beautifully, and with two splendid wheels to bear it whither its constructor willed. Soon after dawn the caravan was hitched on to the Landrover and, to the pleasure of a small gathering of well-wishers and helpers clustered about the gate above Witnesham village, it was drawn sedately out into the lane and off towards the highways and mountain roads of adventure. Giles waved cheerily and Joan smiled enthusiastically. Wasn't life wonderful?

They had reached Derbyshire and were on a main road heading north. There was a fierce wind and driving rain. The caravan, with its considerable side area acting like a sail, had been buffeted and Giles was becoming used to the particular hazard of towing such vehicles. The artist, peering through the deluge which even the windscreen wipers had trouble beating from the glass, had just seen the sign announcing Buxton. There was a horrible lurch and the Landrover was pulled to the right. The caravan had become a dead weight. Giles stopped and, holding a light raincoat over his head, jumped out to inspect the damage. The right wheel had broken, partly disintegrating under the huge burden it had to carry – crates of booze adding considerably to what is referred to in the trade as all-up weight. Giles had miscalculated.

There was to follow a night and day of telephone calls and waiting about in the almost continuous rain, or out of it when possible, in the dry of the now

lopsided caravan. Giles found it difficult to maintain a cheerful, stoical attitude under these circumstances. The fate of Giles's caravan was not quite so drastic as that of Toad's – it will be recalled that this was virtually tipped into a ditch by a speeding road-hog – but there were similarities.

In any event, Giles, who had an impressive degree of influence in the motoring industry, finally took delivery of two lorry wheels the same size as those which had let him down, but of enormous strength. The caravan was never to fail him again.

The same cannot be said for circumstances. One particularly prestigious caravan tour was that of the autumn of 1963. It was to start in the North of England. Plans had been made and designs drawn up for a massive publicity

Giles had arrived in Manchester on 22 November 1963. The Daily Express's *northern edition, printed in that city, was going to announce Giles's forthcoming tour of the area. It was, of course, the day that President John F. Kennedy was assassinated in Dallas, Texas.*

Giles was swiftly removed from the front pages.

Still, a reception party went ahead as Giles and Joan entertained the newspaper's executives in their caravan.

This little doll, a likeness of a Giles cartoon character – George Junior – had been made for the occasion. Here, on that otherwise tragic day, it peeks out of the caravan door with a welcoming smile.

"Caravan? The caravan came off hours ago."

Daily Express, Sept. 11th, 1951

Home! And Ernie lives up to his reputation as that helpful sort of little lad that any family would be blessed to claim as their own. Actually, the caravan was back at the real Giles farmhouse in Suffolk, all ready for a refitting.

launch on the front page of the Manchester editions of the *Daily Express*. There would be Giles and the Family shown setting off and an invitation to readers to join in *en route*. The northern editor, John Buchanan, a bespectacled, hard-smoking and -drinking, old-fashioned newspaperman, had arranged for a reception party and an all-evening drinking session to follow the arrival of the caravan. Even a Giles Family cloth doll of George Junior had been commissioned to boost all the hoo-ha.

As Giles pulled into the car park of Manchester's great black-fronted *Daily Express* building, both he and Joan were aware of a sense of drama and activity. Even in the newspaper's vanway there seemed to be an unusual degree of tension.

Giles stopped where he would spend the night, over in a corner of the lot, so that the other cars of reporters and photographers might come and go freely. Where was everybody? he wondered. Where was the reception? There was something not quite

"Father, dear, let's be honest—let's admit that we haven't the call of the sea in our veins."

Daily Express, July 5th, 1949

As an island nation, we really should be better at it. Navigational horrors aside, this cartoon offers us the definitive study of George the bookworm. He has not the faintest idea of what day it is, let alone that he is about

to be buried under twenty tons of bridge.

But he is a game chap, after a fashion. He always makes the token gesture towards joining in the fun. Here he has simply removed his shirt.

right. Giles glanced at the ship's clock on the wall. It was 6.10 p.m. The date was 22 November. He switched on the radio.

'It has now been confirmed from Dallas, Texas,' read the newscaster, 'that President Kennedy has been shot ...'

Even the great Giles quickly realised that the chances of his Family tour of the northern parts of

the UK dominating the front page of the *Daily Express* the following morning were somewhat less than evens. Grandma and the kids, important as they were in national life, would have to set off on their holiday with only a passing mention. That was life. That was newspapers.

The strange caravan nevertheless gradually became known throughout the land. *Express* readers, in

"This type of craft, sir, is very simple to handle—from the look of things it need be."
(Norfolk Broads)

Daily Express, June 7th, 1951

There is something particularly depressing about the suburban English on do-it-yourself boating holidays.

particular, would watch out for it and at each stop dignitaries would arrive, mayors and self-important chairmen of companies, MPs and police inspectors, sports celebrities, headmasters and scout-masters, clothing-store managers and vicars, sometimes a bishop, and everyone else who felt that they should be seen to be present at such a grand event. All would crowd into the caravan and take advantage of the ever-flowing Giles hospitality.

And thus, three times a week, it would be the Family – Grandma, Vera, the twins, Father, Mother and George the bookworm – whose adventures would be recorded in the pages of the *Daily* and *Sunday Express.* At each watering hole they would bundle out of the caravan and make the best of the new location, whether it be Mousehole in Cornwall, Manchester, or the Forth Bridge.

During the long, dark days of winter, Giles would take them all home.

But on one occasion he stopped off at Ascot, parking his caravan for a week in the huge lot, not far from the racecourse, which was the wintering place and main headquarters of the great Bertram Mills Circus.

The dream of Vera . . . on a Penzance beach.

Daily Express, Aug. 28th, 1951

It is rewarding to know that Vera has such a fertile imagination. Most interesting of all is her fantasy concerning the fate of her husband. Even decapitated, he seems to be entirely unconcerned.

"As a matter of fact we do not think this is better than taking one of those chancy holidays in the Med."

Sunday Express, July 28th, 1974

Grandma on the bog! And, inevitably, Stinker – first-rate news photographer that he is – is there to record what will be one of the more entertaining and certainly less tasteful snaps in his album. He would have seen the wind tugging at the canvas loo's guy ropes and, as they say in the trade, 'set up his shot'. Giles adored Stinker.

"Can you and me reach a pay-agreement with a condition that you join the seamen's strike immediately?"

Sunday Express, August 14th, 1960

Grandma's hat is airborne again and gone forever. She's lost thousands.

"Funny, it looked much bigger at the Boat Show."

Sunday Express, January 12th, 1975

Giles adored boats. He always shows the Family as helpless mariners in scrappy little vessels. There is probably a touch of nautical snobbery in his view of little sailors. Giles owned a magnificent ocean-going yacht and wore a captain's cap to go with it. As with cars and caravans, he was just a shade like Toad of Toad Hall. Still, he was certainly respected as a man of the sea. Ask any waterside tavern on the estuaries of East Anglia.

"You might have let him hit one as it's Father's Day."

Sunday Express, June 18th, 1972

Yes, Father does wear a knotted handkerchief on his head. Is there anywhere else in the world, apart from England, where men on holiday actually sport this particular style of headwear?

"Hear that, everybody? If some of you don't start enjoying yourselves Father won't bring us again next year."

Sunday Express, August 26th, 1979

Rain again! Wind again! And off goes Grandma's hat again! Incidentally, the sign on the side of the café is not entirely an invention of the artist. Once, after tasting revoltingly weak tea in a roadside establishment in Suffolk he featured the premises in this cartoon. He had cheekily written on a sign by the door of the café – 'Guaranteed 200 cups of tea per T bag.' He has never, to this day, dared return to the place.

"Dad'll get 'Fishermen of England' when he arrives home two hours late."
(St. Ives, Cornwall)

Daily Express, Aug. 24th, 1951

You can tell that they are Cornish fishermen. And here Giles gives a splendid plug to a real pub and its obviously real publican. There are many taverns throughout the country which have been thus honoured.

"Tea's ready, Don Juan!"
(Cornwall)

Daily Express, Aug. 25th, 1951

Poor Father. Here he is in the middle of what might be politely termed a midlife crisis.

"There'll be some hollering when we get in—I locked Grandma in the bathroom before we went away."

Sunday Express, Aug. 11th, 1957

Now this is one of those Giles cartoons which, if thought about, is really quite shocking. Judging by the size of the suitcases, the Family has been away for weeks.

Giles, who loves the darker side of comedy, could occasionally show an almost gruesome display of humour. Heaven help the one who opened the bathroom door.

dear all,

plodding north through rain hail hurrycanes and fog to find out what mr ailsham oggs doing about bringing prosperity to the north we found a little hole in the clouds clear enough to show us we were miles off the main road on top of a darbyshire hill

my picture shoes:
1. mr giles telling george he don't think george is a very nice navigator.
2. mrs giles saying she's had all she wants of ailsham oggs bells.
3. auntie vera wimpring because there isn't a kemist in sight.
4. auntie vera's baby wimpring.
5. grandma stretching her legs and saying she don't think much of the mod. con.

6. larry souvineer hunting.
7. the dogs just been told we don't want a lot of noise.
8. vulchers.
more next week i'm afraid.

yours truly,
giles junior.

Daily Express, November 23rd, 1963

Heading north again in the caravan.

"Dad's getting on well with the neighbours, Mum."
(New Forest)

Daily Express, Sept. 7th, 1951

The Giles Family discover what real caravanning is all about.

Giles loved circus people and dispatched his Family into their midst, seeing – rightly – enormous potential for cartoon fun in and about the sawdust ring of one of Britain's noblest traditions.

Circus people adored Giles and his creations. The Family, after all, was precisely the audience for whom they played all of their lives. There, in the front row by the edge of the ring, would be the kids and Grandma, and Uncle and Mother and Father.

Says the artist:

They were travelled and they knew about life. They knew ordinary people. They knew the hardships, but they especially understood the humour. We got to know them all. They would come to our caravan, which was in amongst all

of their caravans, of course, at any time. Ours especially fascinated them because of the room falling out of the side. Almost every performer must have dropped in to see us at some time or other. Trapeze artists, the two midgets, a girl with marvellous performing poodles, the Bertram brothers themselves – wonderfully funny men – and old Coco the clown. Coco's daughter, Olga, was married to Alex Kerr, the lion trainer. He became an especially good friend for years afterwards, and brought a tiger up to the farm in Suffolk for the day.

And so Giles took his own act around the country. Not all of his holiday cartoons featured the caravan, but it was always there – somewhere – out of sight. It

THE GILES FAMILY, circus-bound, in theeir studio-caravan, have been fog-bound, ice-bound, but have at last reached the circus winter quarters at Ascot where they will be living for a while. Nevertheless, there will be a slight delay with funny jokes about circuses while a certain amount of thawing-out takes place.

Daily Express, Dec. 9th, 1952

Giles loved the circus. During the winter of 1952 he parked his caravan, among all the other caravans, at the Ascot headquarters of the Bertram Mills Circus. He and Joan played host to every manner of circus performer, from the midgets and trapeze artists to Coco the celebrated clown.

It was a cold December, as can be judged from his sketch of the Family thawing out.

Giles shares a smoke with the elephant trainer, Mr Gindl. Giles adored 'characters'. He collected them. After he had *befriended the circus people some of them would call at his home outside Ipswich. One even arrived with a tiger.*

"That was a fine idea back at head office telling them to look out for LRT 140 in yesterday's Express . . ."
(Stratford on Avon)

Daily Express, May 9th, 1951

Daily Express readers were always given details of the travel schedule of the caravan. They would arrive in large numbers, some believing that they might, just perhaps, catch sight of Grandma, such was the strange mixture of fact and fantasy which the artist had woven about his now famous odysseys. Crowds would often swarm over the caravan and at times even the Giles's hospitality was stretched to the limits.

'We were sometimes treated as if we were the Beatles,' recalls Giles.

was a kind of travelling Pandora's box, with a door in the side, out of which tumbled and scurried and danced, with their buckets and spades and cheap sunhats and their sandals and sunglasses and tatty little suitcases, the most celebrated ordinary family in the land. Only the most rarified soul has not nudged past them on the promenade, shared a stretch of beach with them or spotted them, preoccupied on a rocky outcrop at the base of some cliff, investigating rock pools and streams and eddies for little critters and creatures to take home in a jar.

But for an illustration of the true mystery of Giles, we could do worse than go to the Gorbals in Glasgow and recall a mysterious event which took place in the fifties when the artist had been visiting Scotland on one of his tours. Giles had parked his caravan by the front door of the *Daily Express* office on the edge, as it was, of the roughest part of that rough city.

One by one, from the side streets, there came young children. They seemed to have been attracted from afar and arrived from all directions. There were girls and boys, most with dirty faces. They were roughs and scruffs, one with a tricycle, one with a home-made board on wheels, another with a catapult, another holding an old tyre. One held his baby brother higher so that he could see, and there was even a baby in a pram.

Soon there were no fewer than fifty of them. They swarmed over the Landrover and tugged at Giles's

A Bertram Mills elephant pays a call on Giles at his caravan door.

expensive white suit. He was jostled and surrounded, almost overwhelmed.

He was for the moment the Pied Piper who had called with his magic pipe to those young and not so innocent folk who eternally inhabit and enthusiastically terrorise that timeless place called Gilesland.

The strangest caravan incident occurred in the notorious Gorbals in Glasgow. Children, none of whom had any idea what the caravan was for, assembled from the side streets. They came from everywhere, in ones and twos and little groups. One small girl carried a baby.

It was as if Giles, like the Pied Piper, had summoned them with his magic to this most unlikely of enchanted places.

CHAPTER FOUR

The Giles Family in Foreign Lands

Giles sat in his cabin on the *Queen Mary* mesmerised by the strangely changing view through the porthole. For what seemed an age he saw merely a perfect circle of light blue Atlantic sky. It seemed, for a while, that the ship might be sailing at a steady forty-five-degree list. Then, finally, the straight edge of the ocean's horizon appeared at the bottom of the round window and rose, quickly filling the porthole with a deep green-blue. This colour, too, remained for a longer time than seemed natural. Would the vessel roll over? Would it just go on until it turned turtle? After an eternity, the light blue circle returned, the ocean sliding down out of sight as if draining from a fish bowl, and Giles was once again gazing at the sky.

This agreeable phenomenon is something which amuses us all when we first go to sea in an ocean liner, but it was particularly intriguing to Giles. It appealed to his vivid cartoonist's imagination. 'I could have watched it for hours,' he recalls. 'The movement of this massive liner, with its dark blue hull, its white superstructure and its great scarlet funnels, could all be imagined just by staring at this circle in the wall of the cabin.'

It was 1948. Carl Giles had earlier been summoned to the grand Fleet Street office of his editor, Arthur

Christiansen. The door shut behind him and Giles was asked to sit down.

'We would like you to go to America,' he was told. 'Go wherever you like – coast to coast – have fun – take as long as you like, spend what you like – and take your wife, Joan.

'We would just like a regular report of your travels through cartoons, of course. And take the Family.'

Giles's temples drummed with excitement. He looked at the large map of the world on the wall of the office. His eyes found the tiny cluster on the edge of the European continent which was the United Kingdom, and moved west across the Atlantic. Could this be happening? His only travels had been to France during the war, as a cartooning correspondent for the *Daily Express*. He had known Americans, particularly those black GIs from the East Anglian air base whom he had befriended in his home county of Suffolk, but America itself had always been a distant, inaccessible place holding the promise of an almost indescribable magic.

So here he was, sailing west to the New World, in a first-class cabin on A Deck of the magnificent *Queen Mary*. His pretty wife Joan was with him, radiant with pleasure and with the happy knowledge that she had a fine wardrobe of frocks for every

"That's handy . . . you've left the iron on, Vera's glasses gone overboard, and Grandma's sulking because they don't sell bulls'-eyes in the Queen Mary."

Daily Express, June 4th, 1948

Giles, with Family, heads for the United States. It was his first trip to that country, even though he had always loved America and admired Americans. He had befriended many of them in East Anglia during the war years, and his famous cartoons of GIs were adored by the American forces. He liked the Yankee brashness and humour.

occasion, pressed and fresh and swinging gently to the roll of the ship behind the mahogany door of the cabin cupboard. Joan, ever practical, was ready for anything, from the captain's table to a barn dance in old Kentucky.

Unseen to those who were not unusually keen of eye there were others who were now exploring this mighty queen of the seas. The occasional glimpse of these figures may have been caught here and there, though it might have been tempting to dismiss it as a trick of the light.

Those many engrossed lovers or dreamy honeymooners strolling along the promenade deck were too intoxicated by the dizzy mystery of each

"Lady, don't keep telling me you think we're being followed by submarines—tell the captain."

Sunday Express, June 6th, 1948

Giles's journey to the States was only three years after the end of the war. The Atlantic had been a place of deadly peril, mainly from German U-boats.

At one stage the Allies were losing 650,000 tons of shipping a month. Now the ocean was once again open, and supporting what was still the most agreeable way to travel in leisure and luxury. Giles describes how he sat mesmerised by the sight of the sea slowly filling up the porthole as the vessel rolled and heaved, and then draining away as if from a goldfish bowl.

others' eyes to notice what could have been an ancient figure dressed in black bombazine, with a hat pulled down over her specs and an umbrella whose handle was ivory and fashioned into the head of a parrot. She had hurried by them, maybe, angrily muttering something about 'seeing the captain'. . .

Accompanying her, possibly, had been a scrawny woman with straight hair whose face had gone as green as the sea and who was picking pathetically at the screw top of a bottle marked 'SQUELLS – seasick pills. Do not overdose'.

The lovers might have noticed a curious-looking fellow in a Frenchman's beret and with a curved meerschaum, leaning on a stanchion. His right hand would have been supporting a book by the philosopher Jean-Paul Sartre. He would have looked so solemnly engrossed in the pages that he could as well have been leaning against a letter-box in Hampstead.

And were those the demonic features of a small child peeking out from under the tarpaulin spread over a lifeboat? And did he have in his hand one of those handles that sailors use to wind the boats clear of the vessel's hull and down into the sea?

All this would have been lost on the passengers. But Giles saw it, of course. Everywhere he went he saw the Family. All of his life's travels, from that time forward, would be in their company. Now, on the *Queen Mary,* he was already bringing them to life in his cabin, on his cartooning paper, as fellow passengers. He was also planning their adventures in America.

Meanwhile, much of Giles's socialising on the ship, despite his celebrity status, soon found a level which would have been understood and appreciated by the members of that cartoon tribe of his imaginings, especially Grandma.

He had been approached by a senior uniformed figure who had almost given a discreet bow and had said respectfully: 'The captain asks whether you would be so good as to join him at his table for dinner.' Giles invited to the captain's table! Giles, once a bespectacled ruffian in the Islington class of that tyrannical schoolmaster Chalkie, was being invited to the captain's table. Now that was something.

And being the captain's table on the *Queen Mary,* it was probably the smartest dining spot, for all of its anti-social heaving and pitching, on any of the planet's seven major oceans. Giles accepted, but he wasn't at all sure that this was to be his natural station in life. Giles was a socialist. He had even, during the early years of the war, when the Germans were hammering the life out of the Russians, professed himself to be a communist. Life's top table was not something he aspired to. He was, later, to become friendly with Royalty and he also became a close chum of Max Aitken, sailing son of his employer, Lord Beaverbrook. But the 'top table', a public perch reserved for the socially elite who should not be seen guzzling with *hoi polloi,* was not a position which gave Giles great comfort. He sat there with white-tied strangers and elegant women in dazzling frocks who held their knives and forks with the delicacy of surgeons wielding scalpels, and who spoke in those sharp-voiced cultured tones that tend to threaten fine glassware.

Grandma, pressing her nose to the salt-encrusted porthole and squinting in the shimmering light of the chandeliers, might have felt inclined to stomp up to the gathering and set about them with her brolly.

It was little wonder that Giles sought a social circle which, in the long hours of the day, restored equilibrium to his egalitarian soul.

This photograph shows Giles in a favoured mode of dress and what was, for a while, a favourite mode of transport. He is seen, wearing a GI's cap and an army-style shirt, sitting soldier-like at the controls of an American jeep.

He was impressed by the American image and couldn't wait to visit the United States.

Here Giles and Joan enjoy dinner on board. They were lured, on occasion, to the captain's table. It was, of course, the most honoured position on the world's most famous ocean liner. But Giles, a Cockney with a taste for material pleasures but a tendency to feel ill-at-ease in posh society, preferred to seek his entertainment elsewhere on the ship.

He eventually found the stewards' quarters, not far above the swill of the bilges. It was there that he did most of his carousing.

"You'd have thought eight million population in New York was plenty."

Daily Express, June 14th, 1948

New York, to those who had endured the blackouts of war days in Britain, had an extraordinary initial impact. It was like some weird and fantastic Gothic city where steam belched from beneath the streets. For Giles it was as if he had stepped into a movie and both he and the Family were dazzled.

"Well, folks—when we arrived from England, Wally pointed out that there were other things in America besides skyscrapers."

Daily Express, Aug. 3rd, 1948

This rather startling cartoon shows a relative of the Family with the American family that her GI husband has brought her to meet. They are, in a way, a hillbilly Family. The cartoonist was amused by the idea that many an English lass marrying an American serviceman might not be entirely prepared for what awaited her on the other side of the Atlantic. There were many cases, on the other hand, of US fathers leaving offspring – some yet unborn – behind. The Family twins, so the artist tell us, are almost certainly a case in point.

Ike, the black GI stationed in Suffolk whom Giles befriended during the war, and for whom he searched in vain in America after the war.

"A pot of tea for three, please."

Daily Express, July 13th, 1948

Giles actually spent some time in the backwoods of America. He searched for the friends he had made among the GIs in Suffolk – particularly his black chums Ike and Butch – but was, sadly, unable to track them down.

He enlisted the help of the Red Cross, but to no avail. Butch and Ike, men whom he had come to love with a great depth, had simply vanished and Giles returned home disappointed.

"Another of Father's bright ideas—'MUST visit a night club before we go back'."

Daily Express, July 3rd, 1948

Giles did have a confrontation with the police in America. He was apprehended for speeding. A huge highway patrolman escorted the bespectacled Englishman across an eight-lane highway which thundered with Leviathan trucks in order to point out a stop sign. They walked back, perilously, to the car where Giles did not, so he recalls, show the required amount of comprehension. 'Follow me,' instructed the cop. The whole procedure was then repeated.

'I found out where the stewards used to do all their drinking,' he recalls. 'It was right down in the bowels of the ship, down where the engines sounded like thunder and where it was hot and there was a powerful humming of the electrics. No other passengers went down – this was decidedly below stairs.'

And thus it was, sharing his time uncomfortably with the posh (port out, starboard home) lot, and

"For goodness sake, Vera, stop worrying about England and the Russians and relax."

Daily Express, July 9th, 1948

Poor Vera. We can only hope there is a place awaiting her in a Giles heaven of some kind. This scene reflects the astonishment with which Giles regarded the deserts of the American Southwest. You know they're there, but they always come as a surprise to those who have perceived America as a land of skyscrapers.

enjoyably with the lads below, that Carl Giles travelled to America. Even he, despite his natural attraction to the United States and to its glamorous, honest, noisy and extrovert people, did not expect to be quite so overwhelmed as he was by his first impression of that astonishing country, especially by his first glimpse of Manhattan.

The artist stood in Times Square and gazed about him. The war was not long over and England had been a place of black-outs. One thing which particularly distinguished a European city at war in those days of bombing raids was not merely the lack of general lighting, but of the neon dazzle of advertising. There was nothing, perhaps, that exploded on the senses of those post-war first-time travellers to America as much as this flashing, vulgar and extravagant, though undeniably exciting, tribute to the excesses of New World capitalism.

Giles was in awe. As was the Family. Indeed, Giles's leisurely tour of the United States, where his ordinary characters from ordinary suburbia in an England still partly numbed by the Blitz and by rationing, gave an enormous boost to his followers. For Giles had shown an England at war where the Americans, in the form of his celebrated cigar-chomping, taxi-hogging GIs, had partly amused the beleaguered Brits, partly irritated them, and yet made them yearn for that world of skyscrapers and neon and nylon stockings. Now he had taken the Family – the ordinary Briton's family – over the sea and shown them the sights.

As the years passed, America became more and more accessible to the lower-middle-class and even working-class Briton and today you will see the Giles Family asking policemen the way on Fifth Avenue, wearing cowboy hats in the Midwest or eating picnics on the edge of the Grand Canyon. They appear everywhere, from Miami to Alaska.

The Giles tour of America lasted two months. It must have cost Father, if it was he who was paying, a fortune. Considering that there were around a dozen heads to be accommodated on pillows and a dozen associated bottoms to be placed on the seats of Greyhound coaches and what-have-you, such a holiday would only be accessible to those who had won the football pools. Where did the money come from? Father goes off to a mysterious job each day, but we never assume it's any more rewarding than that of a manager of some kind, or the boss of a small DIY store. Did Grandma rob a bank? In which case, why weren't we told?

It is an unfair question, of course. Explains Giles: 'That is something you don't ask. But I suppose the fact is that I was lucky always to have enough money not to worry about it, and so it never occurred to me that the Family should have those kinds of problems either.'

We had best think of them as we do of that other prominent family, the Royals. After all, we never see them handling money. It is a commodity, one way and another, which the mighty and the immortal take for granted. And which they never – unless it's Grandma betting at the racecourse or holding up a petrol station – personally handle.

They certainly would have needed it for another regular transatlantic holiday destination – Bermuda. Now there, even today, you would be unlikely to find many families similar to the Giles lot. Bermuda remains one of the most upmarket and expensive island colonies in the world. It is a sub-tropical, closely arranged archipelago twenty miles square, with beaches of sand as fine as icing sugar, aquamarine waters graced with the deep purple of thriving reefs, lush and exotic flora supporting glorious songbirds and white-roofed, rich-man's houses in every colour of an unreal pastel rainbow.

Bermuda is certainly not the place where you would expect to find a socialist cartoonist, nor the earthy, twelve-strong suburban Family of his creation. But there you are. It is best not to apply to the Giles Family what young George would refer to as 'rools'. What is certain is that Giles and his entourage took a great delight in this millionaire's paradise and visited Bermuda regularly. In July 1967, Giles recalls, they arrived on the island in pouring rain. The artist promptly sent a cartoon home showing Grandma being greeted in a monsoon at Bermuda's airport and subsequently, fully clothed and with brolly up for stability, swimming underwater with disconcerted-looking tropical fish in order to avoid the downpour.

Giles was given a generous welcome in Hollywood, particularly by the British. However, the half-naked Tarzan, Lex Barker, looks completely mystified.

(OPPOSITE) *Here, Carl and Joan Giles talk to Sir Ralph Richardson on Paramount Studios' set of* The Heiress. *One of the cartoon twins was named after eccentric motorcycle-riding Sir Ralph. Did he know?*

The family returned to England today. The U.S.A. have since recovered.

Daily Express, Aug. 5th, 1948

George the bookworm becomes more intriguing the more you study him.

(OPPOSITE) *The most unlikely spot on the planet for a Giles Family holiday must be Bermuda. This extraordinary colony, a subtropical millionaires' heaven, where cocktail parties continue round the clock and sun-tanned escapees from the bustling world of distant continents gather on trim lawns beneath palm trees, is about as far from English suburbia as can be imagined.*

Nevertheless, Giles chose it for a vacation. And being a decent sort of chap – and mindful that he should sing for his supper – he took the Family along to keep him company. In the event, he prevailed upon Giles Junior to do the work for him.

Giles Junior sent a note back to readers in England: 'Dear all, all the family are having a high old time here in Bermooda except mum dad auntie vera and granma. hope its raining your end. Yours truly, giles junior.' Actually, the last word had been spelt JUNOR, and an 'i' had been inserted between

124

dear all,

everybody here's lobster pink and getting ready to fly off home and looking forward to all the ultimatums and Rodesian Crisises and emergencys on the Parkistan and football fronts.

mr giles issued an ultimatum that if we dont find granma's hat and aunty Vera's glasses in 2 minutes a state of war will exist between him and us right quick. The twins buried granmas' hat and aunty Vera's glasses so that when they get home they can say they've got property in Bermooda.

Tally O,

your's truly,
giles junor.

dear all,
all the famly are having a high old time here in
bermooda except mum dad anutie vera and
granma.
hope its raining your end.
yours truly,
giles junior.

Giles Junior is possibly the most perplexing member of the Family. He is also known as George Junior and appears to be the baby of the sickly Vera. But he is simply minded by the poor woman, so it seems, until required to stand in for his creator. He then becomes Giles Junior and takes up his pen.

the 'o' and 'r' as an apparent correction. Giles's editor on the *Sunday Express* was the formidable Scotsman John Junor, now Sir John and ever known, both in fear and affection, as 'J.J.' Carl Giles always knew how to keep his employers happy. He was a master at that subtle style of flattery, the kind that only those who enjoy almost impregnable success dare use, known as 'taking the gentle mickey'.

Meanwhile Giles himself was proving, when interviewed by an unsuspecting Bermuda reporter, as grumpy and evasive as ever when it came to enquiries about his private life and the origins of his talent.

Asked the journalist from the *Sun Weekly:* 'Did you learn to draw at school?'

Replied Giles: 'At my school, in the rural district of King's Cross and Islington, the only art you learned was the art of self defence, and I didn't pick up much of that.'

The reporter, in the light of this startling answer, was then rash enough to ask, 'Do you not think that you make children look worse than they really are?'

Said Giles, predictably and gloriously perverse as ever: 'I think I flatter children. They are certainly more anti-social and dangerous than I show them.'

To be just, the choice of Bermuda as a holiday location was very much the exception rather than the summer rule; most of the Giles holidays, which were so fully chronicled and illustrated in the *Express*, were taken closer to home, in France, Italy and Spain. It was Spain, in particular, with which less wealthy readers could identify.

Everybody went to Spain. It was where you discovered post-war sunshine and that intoxicating refreshment which until then had been merely the nectar of the privileged – wine. Spain was to become, for a while, the cheapest place in the world in which to get sloshed and suntanned.

While the Giles Family got stuck in to a round of bullfights, sand and *sangria,* their mentor did things in his usual style. He roared about Spain, wife Joan in sunhat and dark glasses beside him, in his white roadster XJ 120.

Here again, considering that the country was ruled by the fascist General Franco and that it was still a desperately poor nation, the sight of socialist Giles in his white racing car scattering the peasants and the pigs and the chickens was not one which called to mind a hero of the world's downtrodden. Still, Giles, who happily admitted that he could never understand why his own left-wing sympathies should lead him to a life of self-deprivation, was in no way coy about his spectacular methods of travel.

There was one particular cartoon, for example, which not only boasted of the 'XJ' but interestingly created, once again, a bizarre confusion between Giles's actual life and that of his fictional Family. For Giles purists it makes an intriguing collector's item.

The Jaguar is seen being stripped by a team of uniformed officials in the customs shed prior to being driven on to the ferry. The car's owner is quite clearly Father. He is looking crumpled and harassed and is speaking to a lady with a hat-box and small suitcase who is quite plainly Mother. The incident in reality didn't take place, but Giles was always prepared for it.

It is a law in Gilesland that one should be able to jump back and forth between the real and the unreal. It is the same privilege enjoyed by Alice who, after all, simply steps through a looking-glass.

Giles and his Jaguar, however, did come to genuine grief while in Spain.

He remembers the incident with pain. 'It was somewhere in a small place near Madrid and we had been driving on a very hot bright day. I drove slowly into this town and suddenly came out of the brilliant sun and into dark shadow. I was temporarily blinded and there was a horrible crunch. My heart sank. Even the slightest mark on the car gave me sleepless nights.'

"If your swim suit HAS come off in the water, Vera, you'll probably have to stay in until Spain has a change of government."

Sunday Express, June 21st, 1953

Postwar Spain became the most popular holiday destination for the ordinary English citizen. It was amazingly cheap and it was where the British discovered wine. For the aficionados *it was a nation of charm, character and fascinating history. For the rest, it was where you went to get tanned and blotto. Nude bathing was a depraved practice for which the British were well noted.*

"They said, 'Anything on board there shouldn't be?' and for a joke I said, 'Only the Crown Jewels,' so for a joke they said, 'O.K. there's five minutes before your ship leaves—let's have her down to make sure.'"

Daily Express, May 18th, 1953

Here we have an interesting example of how the two worlds of Giles – the real and the imaginary – become entwined. Giles would take his beloved Jaguar XJ 120 on his tours of the Continent and would, as always, find the authority vested in customs men profoundly annoying. He hated piffling bureaucracy.

However, it is not Giles himself who is having to deal with this situation, but Father. The notion of Father owning one of the world's most expensive sports cars is plainly absurd.

"The sooner this family learns that NO ENTRADA on a door in Spain means NO ENTRY the better."

Daily Express, June 25th, 1953

Giles, who counted farming among his accomplishments, has a notably unsentimental attitude to such Walt Disney creatures as ducks and rabbits. He was asked what he thought of bullfighting. It was encouraging to learn that he disapproved. Note Vera's bottle of gippy-tummy pills. It is astonishing, on reflection, that they persuaded her to attend such a frightening event especially as the outcome was bound to be disastrous.

As townspeople gathered round, Giles, already in the depths of misery, peered at the damage. He had struck a lamp post and crumpled one of those famous streamlined headlamps.

Giles prodded it with his finger and picked little triangles of glass from the light's rim. This was it. The holiday was ruined. Further joy was out of the question.

One of the crowd was a small chap in overalls. He looked at the damage and spread his palms as if to say:

'No problem. I will fix it.' Giles looked even more miserable. The idea of a mechanic from a small garage on the road to Madrid 'fixing' his XJ 120 was a dismal prospect. He was wrong. The garage man worked for the whole of that Saturday and Sunday, beating out the metal with thousands of tiny taps of the hammer. Giles had called the boss of Jaguar himself, Bill Lyons, and a new light rim and fitting were swiftly dispatched.

Within two days the 'XJ' was looking as good as new.

130

"It's like this, Mother. I thought I'd step up the travel allowance by running a book on the Derby. Unfortunately they all seem to have backed the winner."

Sunday Express, June 7th, 1953

That celebrated British sporting event, Derby Day, is not forgotten, even amid the madness of Spanish hols.
The Spanish were obviously very up to date on form.

The newly knighted Gordon Richards, riding the 5-1 favourite Pinza, had won his first Derby at the twenty-eighth attempt.

"Before we start—someone can get it into his head that we are not going to have a running commentary of his adventures in France during World War 1."

Daily Express, May 29th, 1950

This remark of Mother's – should some simple mathematics be applied – raises thought-provoking questions about Father's age. In Gilesland it is best not, *perhaps, to dwell too long on such questions as the passage of time and mortality. Neither thing exists, after all, in this timeless place.*

"So far George's immaculate French has got us frogs' legs every time we've ordered steak and chips."

"You English?"

Daily Express, May 29th, 1950

That almost eternally silent thinker, George, appears to have attempted a few words in French – with the degree of success that might have been expected – while his wife Vera receives what could be the hint of a proposition, the only such advance she has had since her pipe-smoking husband asked for her delicate hand in what turned out to be the most depressing state of matrimony known to Little England.

"Les Anglais—they are so shy!"

"Lady in the black hat there—just a moment."

Daily Express, May 29th, 1950

The offer of sex, French-style, causes terror, and Grandma is nicked.

Says Giles: 'The car was back in showroom condition. That little man had been a genius. When I saw the car finished it was the happiest day of my life.'

And so the Gileses set off for the Spanish highway. And whether we were to assume it was Father and Mother, Grandma and the rest of the mob who crammed themselves into this precious car or whether it was just Giles and wife Joan, it mattered not. Everyone was happy again!

This was not to be the first occasion that the Gileses and the Family, between them, were to become the centre of Spanish attention. Mr and Mrs Carl Giles were, aside from their habit of travelling in the 'XJ', a self-effacing and immaculately behaved pair of tourists. But if the Family settled down for a pavement meal there was always a terrible scene. Their appearance on the beach brought Franco's soldiers to the cliff-tops, fearful of riotous behaviour, and alerted by the word, which had spread along the coast, of Grandma's threat to swim in the buff. Inevitably, too, the Family visited the bullfight and found themselves in the ring.

Wherever they went abroad, the Family managed to cause some sort of kerfuffle. It was that old British travelling problem which arises from a certainty that one is, at any given moment in the odyssey, the centre of affairs; that the town, village or quayside has been awaiting one's arrival, and that everything should stop in its tracks at the appearance of one's party, that tables should be made available, that sun awnings should be pulled out and that everyone should miraculously start to speak English.

Here, again, Giles and his wife, Joan, deviated from the stereotype. Neither spoke any French, Spanish or Italian whatsoever, but they never suffered embarrassment nor wanted for anything. Giles kept a small collection of colouring pencils in his pocket, and whenever he needed anything he would simply take a neat little pad and draw his request – be it for toothpaste, a three-course meal or an elastic band.

In restaurants waiters gathered round in wonderment. Giles drew bread, brown or white, did a marvellous 'beef' – a bull – and took only a second to draw a fried egg. 'I just did a little circle and put a pale yellow spot in the middle of it.'

But there were complicated orders which took a little longer. As Giles drew, selecting pencils from his little bunch, the waiters peered down, clutching their napkins, in fascination.

What was this? *Ah, oui! Escargot, monsieur! Magnifique!*

However, Giles reserved his masterpiece for Italy. Spaghetti!

And so, while the master entertained the locals with his artistry, his famous Family toured the world, making a spectacle of themselves and, through the regular pictorial diary of their adventures, causing enormous amusement back home.

'Thank God we're not like that,' the less perceptive would say. Some knew better, of course. For Giles's Family, as ever, was representing them – from Bromley to Eastbourne, from Edgware to Cockfosters – to perfection.

CHAPTER FIVE

The Giles Family at Home

It was wartime and Giles was living in his farmhouse near Ipswich. He dispatched his cartoons to London three times a week but seldom travelled to the capital. Giles had wished to join the army, but the deafness which he had suffered since a motor-cycle accident when he was seventeen prevented him from taking a warrior's role. So at this time, and before he was sent to France with a brief to cover the progress of the war with his pencil and sketch pad, his principal association with the conflict was his friendship with a number of GIs, mostly black, who were building runways on the East Anglian bomber bases.

These massive, dark-skinned soldiers would stay with the Gileses at their home, startling the villagers, and particularly the milkman and the postman and those other regular callers, who had never seen a black man in the flesh. Some were musicians and, in time, with the multi-talented cartoonist playing the piano, the group formed a Dixieland-style jazz band. The drummer was a stout-hearted, gentle, smiling fellow called Butch.

One day, while the GIs were staying at the farmhouse in Witnesham, Giles and Joan took delivery of a black spaniel puppy. The creature was the immediate centre of attention and, while Giles himself had always taken a less than sentimental view of animals, the huge American visitors were utterly intrigued, spending much time on the floor playing with the animal.

During the evening the house party set off in a couple of motor cars to Giles's tavern, The Fountain. The band had assembled at the piano, surrounded by the usual fascinated group of beer-drinking locals, when it was discovered that Butch was missing. Realising that he must have been left behind, as someone often is when more than one motor car is involved in transporting a disorganised party from A to B, Giles drove back to the farmhouse.

There, he found Butch in the kitchen, sprawled on the floor stroking the puppy. When the rest of the household had left, the dog had started to whimper; and big Butch, oblivious of the move to the pub, had stayed back to comfort it.

The pup had had no name until that moment. From then on he was called – inevitably – Butch.

Over the next fifty years, the Gileses were to have a number of Butches, and they keep the tradition to this day. As each Butch has expired – they all died of old age – so another Butch has replaced him. The last three have been Airedales.

While dogs of other breeds have made appearances, it is an Airedale Butch that, having long featured regularly in the cartoons, has now become a member of the Family.

"Dad, you know the Consumers Association said a goose is a better guard dog than a dog?"

Daily Express, November 24th, 1981

Butch shared his strange life between Gilesland and the real, rural world of the cartoonist's Suffolk farmhouse. He wandered between the two. Giles and Joan kept a succession of real doggies called Butch over many years, acquiring a new dog as each died of old age. However, in his cartoon existence, the animal was simply and mysteriously reincarnated. In this sense the dog was given the gift of immortality by his powerful master.

"You're not sending him back to Harridges to change them all on his own?"

Daily Express, December 30th, 1982

Butch attached himself to Grandma and she often seemed to be the only member of the Family who would take much interest in him. Here he has been given the unhappy task of changing a pair of the old besom's slippers, purchased in the sales. Where, one wonders, might Harridges be? Not in Knightsbridge, surely?

"Dad, have a look and see if my tortoise is awake now summer time's started."

Sunday Express, March 19th, 1972

Another truly magical place was the shed in the Giles Family's suburban back garden. It changed shape frequently and would transform itself from a neatly appointed workshop to a store for junk. It also housed various animals, including Ernie's tortoise – winter quarters – and, on occasion, a colony of hedgehogs.

"Of course, you realise that if my Dad gives it up we shall have to start buying our own."

Sunday Express, June 30th, 1957

The other astonishing property of the Giles Family shed was the space inside. Rather like the famous telephone box in television's science fiction series, Dr Who, it expanded once you were within it to grand and amazing proportions.

Incidentally, Giles may well feel that the topic of smoking is less than comical these days. He was almost a chainsmoker for much of his life and the addiction led to serious circulation problems.

But Butch shares his canine existence between the real world and the fantasy world, living both at the farmhouse in Suffolk and in the Family's home in suburbia. However, in the timeless world of the Giles Family, the spirit of one dog, as it were, always passes seamlessly to the next. In that sense, Butch was given, by his Master, the glorious gift of true immortality.

There is little doubt that Butch preferred his true existence up in East Anglia to that of his cartoon life. In the one place he had the run of a farm; in the other he dwelt, always in some kind of mortal danger, at the centre of anarchy. The safest place seemed to be under Grandma's chair, though even that haven was often subject to terrorist activity of some kind. Grandma at least took him for walks. Indeed, it might be said that Grandma was, on the whole, the only one who paid regular attention to him.

Night-time must have been a blessed relief, though where everyone slept in the Family's semi is another one of those mysteries which it is unwise to probe too deeply. Giles himself suggests that the young all slept in one bed, with just their heads poking above the blanket, and the twins in the middle.

But that leaves Mother and Father, the two girls, George the bookworm, Vera and Grandma. There must have been, at the very least, five bedrooms. If there were fewer, then – after lights out – the Family household must have resembled some hideous, overcrowded slum dwelling. But we know that is not the case. The Family was not short of a bob and always had enough money to travel and enjoy life.

So where, if we must, do we place them? Are they working class, upper working class, lower middle class or, perhaps, even middle class?

Suggests celebrated novelist, playwright, columnist and man of letters Keith Waterhouse, himself a working-class Yorkshireman: 'It is curious. I think they are probably a working-class family living a middle-class lifestyle. They are pipe-smoking and pints – not Scotches and vodkas.'

Another distinguished working-class commentator, the Cockney writer and jazz critic Benny Green, agrees:

The Giles Family are downmarket for that house. Definitely. Giles got the working class right. Having lived in the back streets, I know. You always saw the Giles lot – or people like them – sitting outside pubs in the evening. There would be Father and Mother – and very often there would be a battleaxe of a grandma looking ferocious.

In the working classes in those days no one had a house, no one had any money. There were families of twelve all living together and there was that complete lack of privacy – just as there seems to be in the Giles Family household.

It always looked to me as though the Gileses were living above themselves. It looked as though they had come good in some way – won the pools maybe. But I must say that they are quite different in some respects. Father and Mother would usually lash out all the time. You would get a wallop. A thick ear. You don't see that in the Giles household – maybe they have just been overwhelmed by the sheer tyranny of the young. Then if a couple of kids went missing, that didn't matter too much, there were always seven others. In Giles they are always accounted for.

Giles himself, when he was ten, moved from Islington to Edgware. The decision had been taken by his twenty-year-old brother. It was not a popular one, but his brother, not much liked by the young Giles, seems to have taken control of this rather gentle family. What he said prevailed. The real Giles family home, in Islington, was a Victorian house

"Dad—what's it worth if we don't tell Mum you've forgotten Mother's Day?"

Sunday Express, April 1st, 1962

Mother's Day and Father's Day are two of the principal festivals in this household. They are, without fail, events of the most appallingly unspeakable misery for those whose anything-but-blessed existence is celebrated.

143

"Well children, did you have a nice ramble?"

Sunday Express, May 28th, 1978

Butch has managed to secure for himself a level crossing sign. Giles would have been delighted by this particular piece of vandalism. He hated level crossings and level-crossing keepers as much as he did traffic tickets and traffic wardens. Both, he felt, represented an abominable obstruction to his motoring activities.

Giles's only formal studies in art were evening classes in anatomy. He put such researches to good use here. Still, if the Y-fronts on Michelangelo's David were put there for mischievous reasons – or even just for decency's sake – how did whoever put them there get them on?

It was known well enough that Grandma appeared to have two identical sisters in the North of England. The appearance of another one came as a surprise to many. For here we have a pink Grandma. The label at her feet makes it clear where she comes from. Cork. This astonishingly garbed lady represents the hitherto unknown Irish branch.

(ABOVE) *A Christmas card with an unusual role for Grandma.*

(ABOVE RIGHT) *Stuck again. Another of Giles's ever-popular Christmas cards.*

(RIGHT) *Here is Stinker in benevolent mood again!*

Giles also drew Christmas cards for the Game Conservancy Trust. Stinker has abandoned his camera for a very accurate catapult. Always silent, he is a gifted and deeply mysterious little fellow.

Another for the Game Conservancy Trust. It is difficult to imagine how long it took Giles to draw the fine, complex lines of the elephant's skin. But it is another marvellous example of the life-like detail he brings to his drawings of animals.

The RNLI again!

For the RNLI. Giles has a passionate regard for those who risk their lives to save others on the high seas. He has helped raise more money for lifeboatmen, probably, than for any other organisation.

Another for the RNLI. Saving Natalie the Cat is evidently not the normal kind of rescue operation that this particular coxswain would contemplate.

(OPPOSITE) *Here is Stinker, once again, about to snap the effects of extreme pain with his camera.*

Father's Christmas present turns out to have been an extremely bad idea all round.

"Next one who switches RAWHIDE on in the middle of my Olympic Games—BED!"

Daily Express, August 25th, 1960

The introduction of the remote-control television device must surely have been the most iniquitous development in the progress of that particular medium. From then onwards, suburbia was finally deprived of even that most basically therapeutic form of simple household exercise – 'changing channels'.

where they lived in modest comfort. They never wanted for anything and they all had their own beds. Now, with the move, it was almost a question of commuting. Father Giles went by Tube to his tobacco shops and young Giles walked to school.

'Different school – same hooligans,' remembers Giles.

Giles hated the house in Edgware. He missed the character and life of Islington and loathed the sameness, the lack of contrast and the predictability of suburbia.

In Islington we lived on a square. There was an area of grass in the middle protected by railings. You had a key if you lived round the square and could let yourself in. If you were on your own it was like your own grounds.

There was such a dullness about Edgware. And there was always this comparing of houses. If you had a drive running up the side of your place to a garage then you were something special. If you lived in a corner house, you were in Buckingham Palace.

145

"The electricians' strike doesn't really affect us—Father does all his own electrical repairs."

Daily Express, Jan. 19th, 1954

Giles's timing works wonderfully here. It is not what is happening that causes the alarm, but what is about to happen.

There was a little patch of grass in front of the house and a bigger, rectangular patch at the back. And there was always a little woodshed, of course. I used to spend a lot of time in there. That's where I learned my DIY. I think I still have some of those tools to this very day.

And here it was that the Giles Family's celebrated house, its unchanging home for fifty years, had its origins. Here, season after season for half a century, this complicated and bustling clan have pursued their lives. It has been a corner of suburbia which has had its share of rain and inclement weather, but where every Christmas is white and where a genuine Santa

Claus calls, with fully packed sleigh and sturdy reindeer. He usually, however, finds himself stuck in a chimney after stealing the family silver or, at the very least, spotted by a youngster swigging the booze or stealing the coal during a miners' strike.

The Giles Family have never aged. There have been no births and no deaths. The only evidence of procreative activity is in the simple presence of Family members, and particularly of the illegitimate twins, offspring of some unknown GI long returned to the United States to sire other cartoon children, perhaps.

The notion that George the bookworm and pathetic Vera still enjoy connubial bliss is fairly horrifying, and nice Mother and Father are probably

146

"That's the kind of video nasty I'd ban from the home—two reels of Grandma and Vera paddling in Benidorm."

Sunday Express, November 13th, 1983

Note Carol's ghastly looking boyfriend. Such figures would turn up from time to time, but they never seemed to stay for long. Sitting beside Carol is Bridget. Or should it be the other way around? Printers, somewhere back in time, had confused the two girls in a caption. Thereafter, no one quite knew which was which. Even Giles seems a little perplexed. 'The three sisters started off as A, B and C,' he explains. 'That was to make it easy for everyone to know which was which – Ann, Bridget and Carol, in descending order of age. But there was a mix-up and they never quite recovered from it.' Now Bridget seems to be the youngest.

too exhausted at the end of the day. Carol, it should be said, is occasionally seen with some suitor or other, usually a loutish-looking figure who sprawls uncomfortably on the settee amidst the family chaos. One somehow imagines that petting and fumbling is about all they get up to.

There is little passion of any kind, except in the occasional fury of Grandma. They just seem to get on with it. The lives of the Giles Family, indeed, are entirely absorbed by triviality.

That is not to say that their routine is without its drama or, in one domestic sense, its violence. What we tend to see in one of Giles's freeze-frame pictures, which are like 'stills' in a complicated imagined sequence, is the moment before an event. We observe a scene in the Family kitchen during industrial action by electricians in 1954. Mother, who is pouring the tea for a lady neighbour, explains: 'The electricians' strike doesn't really affect us – Father does all his own electrical repairs.' There is steam coming out of the radio and there is a broadcast from the BBC's old Light Programme coming from the spout of the electric kettle.

As she speaks, Father strikes a live wire in the fuse box and Vera, whose finger is on the light switch and who is carrying one of the twins, also becomes 'live'. Father, with screw-driver still making contact, becomes airborne as Vera is surrounded by sparks and small, jagged bolts of lightning leap from the ears of the twin she holds. It would be easy, at this point, to chuckle at the picture and turn the page.

But no. We would have missed the most significant piece of the action. Grandma is asleep, the paper folded under her motionless hands on her lap. Ernie and George Junior, who enjoy a diabolic partnership, have stripped a couple of inches of flex and attached the naked wire to the toe which is protruding from the black stocking on her left foot. Ernie, his eyes wide with sadistic anticipation, is placing the plug at the other end of the wire into the socket. There is but

a second to go and Grandma will rise into the air – her hair standing on end – screaming blue murder. We imagine that. And it is a vivid picture.

Observes Keith Waterhouse:

They all lead charmed lives – like characters in 'Tom and Jerry'. There the cat gets squashed, stretched, impossibly twisted or blown up by a stick of dynamite, but always recovers in seconds. You see a kid sawing away at a branch up a tree on which his sister is sitting. You imagine the catastrophe, though you don't actually see it. However, no one ever has bandages. They all recover remarkably from what in true life would be the kind of injuries which put you into intensive care or Stoke Mandeville Hospital. Or the morgue. What makes it that bit more horrifying is the realism of the drawing. You really can – in graphic detail – imagine the scene. And then hear the sound of the ambulance coming down that road in Slough or wherever it is.

The odd electrocution apart, the Family's daily activities would be utterly dreary were they to occur to anyone else.

Nicholas Garland, the *Daily Telegraph's* distinguished and rather more serious political cartoonist and lifetime admirer of Giles's work, says:

He deals in minutiae. There are no tragedies, there are no great events. Everything which happens is unimportant. It is all about small domestic issues concerning completely inconsequential figures in whose life nothing happens. It's about getting up and shopping and putting the dog out.

The Gileses live in a dull, boring street in which nothing goes on. But there is this amazing realism. And detail. And humour. And you are fascinated. It was said of Chekhov that he 'held

148

"You might try and look pleased they've won a little pig."

Sunday Express, August 7th, 1966

Here is Giles's famous English summer rain. As with his rendering of snow, it shows his mastery of the art of weather.

"I told him as there's no football he can stay at home and amuse the children."

Sunday Express, January 20th, 1963

It is a notable fact of the Family household that the malevolent children never get swatted. It was a point raised in the context of this collection of cartoons by writer and music critic Benny Green. He found it astonishing that in a working-class household, which he took the Family household to be, the children were allowed to behave so badly without regularly being given a thick ear. The mystery must remain unsolved.

Those who are equally frustrated by the lack of discipline in this home will, perhaps, be delighted by this truly rare Giles cartoon. For here is an occasion when Father has taken suitably drastic action to restrain the little horrors in proper style rather than letting them rampage around him as usual.

"Dad, as a matter of interest, who tied us up?"

Daily Express, June 29th, 1965

Search here for the horrified little official with a loud hailer.

life fluttering in his hand'. That's exactly what Giles does.

I also get the impression that these people are trying to better themselves. They do have a wish to improve their circumstances. In this respect and others Giles's ironic eye gets it absolutely right. Everything of his is so beautifully observed.

"You don't encourage your dad very much telling him that's more than he's scored in his whole life."

Sunday Express, May 8th, 1988

Only the horses for Grandma!

"At least we know now that the Falkland Islands are not the ones north of the Hebrides and the Orkneys are not somewhere off South America."

Daily Express, April 13th, 1982

The cry can occasionally be heard in the cartoonist's Suffolk home: 'Joan, get my gun. There are a couple of bloody rabbits in the flower bed.' Giles will be sitting in his wheelchair at the French windows, fuming and raging over what he considers to be an intolerable invasion of the beautifully trimmed flora of his garden.

Giles has, in days gone by, despatched many a bunny from his hidden vantage point in the sitting room.

However, nowadays no gun is ever forthcoming. Joan has a more tolerant regard for creatures of the hedgerow.

"We've got to sign an agreement that in the event of a future water shortage no way will they have to share a bath with Grandma."

Sunday Express, January 23rd, 1983

The unspeakable implications of the drought!

"Out come the old '39–'45 war jokes—'If you want to help our boys you should send those socks to the enemy'"

Sunday Express, April 25th, 1982

Grandma was always the first to enter into the full spirit of the war effort. It was on 2 April 1982 that the Argentine forces invaded the Falkland Islands. Soon, the Task Force would arrive in the South Atlantic to kick 'em off – with the help, or otherwise, of Grandma's and Vera's socks.

"You say Georgie Smith was showing you how to make H-bombs in the tool shed?"

Daily Express, Feb. 7th, 1950

'President Truman,' read a report, 'today [31 January] gave the go-ahead to the American Atomic Energy Commission to research and produce the hydrogen bomb. It is expected to be 100 to 1,000 times as powerful as the bomb dropped on Hiroshima and Nagasaki.' The threat of a global holocaust had everyone sleeping uneasily in their beds, though George the bookworm seems to be as unperturbed as you would expect him to be.

"I should have thought we could have managed without your contribution to Mothers' Day."

Sunday Express, Mar. 19th, 1950

This is Natalie the Cat. She eventually disappeared. In the cartoonist's home, it was thought that she may have expired, but death does not stalk Gilesland. Natalie had simply, we must presume, wandered off to find a more peaceful place in which to bring up her young – and who can blame her?

Garland also sees the darker side of Giles, that vital element which gives the work a surprising depth, a rich though faintly sinister dimension.

He says: 'His Grandma can be violent, wicked, cynical. She reigns by misrule. She turns everything on its head, though she is an old lady whom you cheer on.

'She routs thugs. She is tough. She doesn't have a

romantic view of anything. She is, in effect, the total opposite, in every respect, to that old roly-poly puff-ball – what's her name?'

'Barbara Cartland?'

'Yes, Barbara Cartland.'

'The kids can be evil, too. They are sadistic.'

'But you know, there is something very touching about Giles's affection for his characters. They have an awareness of melancholy. They have redeeming features. There are many reasons to respect the work of Giles. Not just his characters. The way he deals with weather is amazing. He is the only cartoonist I know, for example, who can successfully draw fog.'

Rain, too. Indeed, the artist loved to subject his Family, regularly, to the most dreadful weather conditions. In December they were always buried in snow. Otherwise it was rain: rain on the cricket ground, rain at the races, rain on holiday, rain at the vicar's tea party. No one but Giles can make a wet English summer afternoon look quite so horribly wet. You can actually feel the water running down the back of your neck.

Study his cartoon of 7 August 1966 (page 149). It may well make you shiver and want to jump into a hot bath before taking tea and scoffing muffins in front of the fire.

There are huddles of unhappy people under the tree, crowded into soggy tents; the banner which joyfully proclaims the Grand Fete, a sign devised with high summer in mind, sags horribly. The vicar is sodden. George the thinker is emptying water out of his pipe.

The Family is drenched. But it is Giles's technique for achieving weather effects with his pencil which makes you feel that you are there. For rain, for example, he leaves the ground undetailed except for those smudgy, watery reflections of the characters. The downpour effect is created with about a hundred angled dashes of the pen. It looks simple. It isn't. How interestingly this particular picture illustrates that one criticism which some students of his work will repeat, though quietly and in carefully chosen company: that the central joke so often threatens to let the cartoon down. Here the joke really isn't very funny at all. But the cartoon is so magnificent in all other respects that it simply doesn't matter.

Wrote art critic William Feaver: 'The excuse for the joke is often less effective than the placing: dour wintry sky over the station approach; mud at low tide; juggernauts churning the slush – no one is more used to conveying in tone and scribble the precise textures of pebbledash and privet.'

Feaver had made a study of the Giles Family and had become an expert on the subject. He wrote in 1985: 'Like the Archers, the Huggets, the Dixons, the Glums, the Garnetts and the Ogdens – who all owe something to them – the Gileses are not so much your typical English family as a family around whom everything revolves. They are provincial but come up to town quite a bit – the Boat Show and so on – and travel a good deal. Their credibility depends largely on the accuracy of the settings.'

Feaver describes one cartoon of Sunday 16 June 1985 which, in contrast to the often prevailing rain and wind, shows the Family in summer mood. The weather is plainly warm, but the event is fraught, as ever, with that discomfort which is their permanent lot. Completely serene happiness, for all of them at any given time, is simply not on the agenda.

Wrote Feaver: 'Dad slips away on his own for a bit of coarse fishing. Hardly has he settled down with thermos and sandwiches in the shade of a burly Giles willow when across the meadow come Mum and Bridget, Ernie sounding the trumpet, the twins with their cymbals, George with baskets, Vera with her hanky and Grandma, ahead of the field in her Sinclair C5. He should have known; it's Father's Day.'

"When I said build them a tree-house to keep them quiet, I didn't mean to include room-service."

Sunday Express, July 24th, 1977

This is a treehouse which would have been the envy of any suburban back garden.

While the Giles Family are restricted to their scruffy patch behind the house, Carl Giles has – in earlier years – actively farmed his own eighty acres. The dog here, a spaniel, was one of the many Butches.

"Assuming their teachers do go on strike and we've got to have them at home a few more weeks . . ."

Sunday Express, April 9th, 1961

Note the object of George Junior's fascination.

These miseries of suburban Family life seem so far away from the pastoral tranquillity of Suffolk. For while Giles knew suburbia when he was a child he has spent the past fifty years enjoying a personal life which is a notable contrast to the anarchical existence of his created Family.

He has lived alone with his serenely loving and long-suffering wife, Joan, in a comfortable, brightly painted, sensibly furnished home. He had converted it himself from a dingy and poky collection of agricultural buildings.

In the place of the little square of grass with the tiny shed in Edgware, he has farmed 80 acres and enjoyed a workshop 100 feet long by 60 feet wide, in which he has built and serviced machinery and created all manner of gadgetry, and carved and crafted woodwork to an amazingly professional standard. He has several garages, converted outbuildings in which he keeps his Bentley, his Jaguar XJ 120, his Landrover and other vehicles.

His sailing activities, too, are somewhat grander than those of the Family. Where they, with the matriarch as captain, splash about the harbour in an unsafe-looking dinghy, he has owned and skippered a number of superb ocean-going yachts, proud and stately craft which have been the toast of the East Anglian mariners' community.

Yet there are days when these two worlds touch. Giles will be in his wheelchair when an unsuspecting rug salesman will put his manicured finger on the bell and press it long and hard. 'Who the 'ell is that?' Giles will roar, his glasses flashing as he turns his head to the door, his features collapsing with rage. Suddenly, with his short white hair, he looks just like Grandma. And he has Grandma's shrewdness, too, of course. He knows from the tone and the ringing time of that bell that it is someone who is selling something unwanted, someone who has outrageously interrupted, with squalid commercial intent, the peace and privacy of the Giles home.

Joan will calmly attend to the caller. 'Tell him to bugger off, whoever it is,' shouts Giles. Suddenly the latest Butch will wake up and, slow to react as ever, make a dash for the door himself. His tail will catch in the telephone wire and the contraption will fly through the air, crashing on to the tea trolley.

And in the midst of it all sister Eileen will arrive.

Tea will be served and Eileen and Joan will attend to Giles's needs. He is still grumpy, perhaps from the recent intrusion at the front door. 'Women, they're all the same,' he will say.

'What have women got to do with it?' Joan will ask as she pours the milk. 'It wasn't a woman, it was a man.'

'Well,' Giles will say. 'If it wasn't for you bloody women, these people wouldn't bother to call in the first place.'

The mood improves suddenly. Giles smiles at his sister, six years his junior. He has always tormented her. And loved her. And she, the passive and patient victim, has always adored him. There has always been something about their relationship which is unmistakably similar to the kind of thing you would find in Gilesland. When Eileen gave birth to her daughter, Giles drew an outrageous private cartoon to mark the event. Eileen had a son of four years old at the time. And as the situation was almost identical to that of Giles's own youth – older brother and baby sister – Giles's drawing featured the little boy swiping his sister for six with a cricket bat. In every respect, it was pure Giles. Now, all these years later, here was Eileen round again, as she was at least once or twice a week, for tea. Giles leans over, as he always does, and pats her affectionately on the knee. 'Hello, mate,' he says.

In a wink, Grandma has vanished.

Johnny Speight, a close friend of Giles's, is always a welcome visitor to the farm and has thus seen Giles in his domestic circumstances. He too believes that Giles and Grandma – for moments at a time – are

162

"Coleridge said it right—'Yea, slimy things did crawl with legs Upon the slimy sea.'"

Daily Express, January 1st, 1958

You couldn't keep Giles away from the Boat Show. He loved everything to do with boats. The splendid, sweeping way in which the artist has drawn this superb hull shows his pleasure in such craft. At different times in his life he had owned two beautiful yachts exactly like it. The cartoonist's craft were in magnificent contrast to the frightful little vessels into which the Family crammed themselves throughout the summer.

one and the same. He wrote in tribute:

The gift that he has is to see us and point out, with wit and humour, that touch that very few have – to mirror what we are. A talent to draw and bring to life ... not only to draw but to know what to draw ... Plus ... that great touch ... the 'common' touch ... the rare ability to reach right across the board. He spots our funny shapes, the nose that doesn't quite fit, the eyebrows that look more like moustaches, and his women who look more like men ... those faces we see in the crowd, those awful relations, those awful neighbours ... and those cats who look far more elegant and superior in shape than their owners and seem to know it. I could go on ... I've known Giles now for many years and have a strong suspicion he is Grandma.

So, Giles created the bustling, chaotic, lawless life of his Family in a tranquil place far from the suburbs, far from Edgware or Orpington. Each morning he rose early. In the summer he was woken up by the undisciplined musical glory of the dawn chorus, and in the winter by the harsh and brutal frenzy of a Smith's alarm clock. He would read the papers for his ideas and drive to his superbly appointed, brightly lit studio four miles away in Ipswich. With the honking of traffic

When Eileen gave birth to a daughter, Tricia, Giles sent her this card depicting the imagined reaction of Eileen's four-year-old son Christopher. It had echoes of the day, presumably, that Eileen herself was born.
In any case, it has that shocking flourish and outrageous sentiment that could only come from the cartooning brush of one artist.

and the occasional wail of a police car only a distant and scarcely noticeable distraction, Giles entered the world of his creation.

He would, like Alice, step through the looking-glass. For many hours he would inhabit that house in Edgware – or wherever it might be – and his characters would simply grow and spiral into life from the end of his magical pencil. He was not merely creating their activities; he was observing them, almost as if he was not entirely involved.

He was, at moments, an onlooker, like the spiky-haired, silent little boy with the camera, Stinker. When you manage to persuade Giles to speak of his Family, he will speak of them as if they were his own flesh and blood. Well, they are, of course. And there is the secret.

As Giles worked away in his Ipswich studio, newspaper executives far away in London were constantly complaining amongst themselves that Giles didn't work where they could keep an eye on him, where – as the deadline approached – they could go in to his office, point at their watches, and tell him he had just ten minutes to go. Some were outraged that an employee should be allowed to 'work at home'. They were even more outraged, and alarmed, that they had to wait each day for the Giles cartoon to arrive at Liverpool Street railway station. Often the drawing was on a later – sometimes much later – train.

Meanwhile the mighty *Daily Express* trembled as the vast machines held back their power, oily Leviathans leashed in and tethered until that messenger from the station had arrived breathless at the editor's door with the package from Suffolk. Great men perspired. Some grew faint at the sheer stress and terror of it all. But no one understood.

Indeed, one of the funnier notes on Giles came from his editor of the time, Arthur Christiansen. Now, here was a boss having to turn all of his journalistic principles topsy-turvy in order to accommodate the great Giles. In the following tribute you can almost detect that he is nearing the end of his tether. He attempts an easy tone, but here is a man desperately trying to keep calm.

He wrote:

> I have only one thing against Giles – he will not work in London. Ever since he joined the Express

Far, far from their young days in suburban Edgware, here are Giles and Eileen, his younger sister. He used to torment her terribly as a child. He still does on occasions.

'Remember,' he says, 'that the contract we had when we were young is still in force.' He refers to the 'arrangement' he had with the Almighty, a pact that God should keep an eye on Eileen and report any of her misdeeds back to Giles. This was a method employed by the mischievous young Carl to insure against being 'told on' at home. It worked. Still does, perhaps.

The pair are seen here in Suffolk.

"Here is a recording made on Budget Day 1957: 'If they put any more on cigarettes, I'm definitely giving them up'."

Daily Express, March 19th, 1985

The evil economy!

organisation he has firmly and successfully resisted my attempts to persuade him to leave his studios in Ipswich.

I see him only once a month on average. For the rest, my business is conducted by telephone.

And Giles in turn telephones to say that his cartoon has been dispatched by a train that will eventually [note that 'eventually'] arrive at Liverpool Street station. You will see, therefore, that I have no hand in the creation of a Giles cartoon. Editors are able to guide and assist many of their contributors, and like the Russians have the right to say 'No'. But Giles has his own operational methods. He is a law unto himself. I usually say 'Yes'.

Now we see Christiansen rationalise it all for what is quite clearly his own peace of mind.

And with the growth of experience of nursing this extraordinary man, I am bound to admit that he is right to shun London. For his genius derives from contact with the people. Not the people of Fleet Street who on the whole are an odd and peculiar tribe, but the simple, solid people who live simple, solid lives and are the backbone of Britain.

Giles's editor on the *Sunday Express,* John Gordon, had a similarly confused view of the man. He saw him as an uncertain, temperamental, awkward figure, given to self-doubt and misery, a crushed individual who shuffled about his country parish studying the peculiarities of human nature.

He wrote of the difficulties of persuading Giles, who had worked happily for the communist Sunday newspaper, *Reynolds News,* to join the *Express.*

I will tell you frankly that the transfer was not an easy matter. Geniuses, as everyone like myself who has to drive a team of them knows, are 'Kittle Cattle', as they say in Scotland. Sometimes you coax them, sometimes you drive them, sometimes they cry on your knee, sometimes they drive you almost to crying on theirs. But by and large they have one attribute in common. At the start, at least, whatever change may come over them later, they are not susceptible to money persuasion. You can't bribe them.

Giles was making very little money indeed. I took the lid off the Aladdin's cave and let him peep in. All he kept saying was: 'I am very happy where I am. I would be very unhappy if I changed.' Well, they say that water wears away a stone. Certainly, it took much water and other liquids to wear down this particular stone, but in the end, as I determined it should be in the beginning, I transferred it from the other brook to mine.

It would probably be true to say, and I think Giles would agree with it, that having made the change he became for a time a very unhappy man. He missed the old familiar faces and the old comfortable setting. He was uncertain, diffident and thoroughly miserable. Then all of a sudden he changed. The old certainty of touch returned. The sad grey eyes began to twinkle again behind the heavy spectacles. One day I heard him laugh uproariously at one of his own jokes. What caused the change? The usual thing. Readers had begun to write to him in masses telling him how much they liked him.

Of Giles's determination to work from Suffolk he took a more relaxed view, though he commented: 'He loathes town and prefers the quieter sociability of Ipswich. All around that town I am told he is a familiar and well-liked figure as he moons about, seeking detail which will one day become part of a cartoon.'

So, we have a picture of a sad, sensitive creature, shoulders hunched, kicking an old boot about wasteland and peering through smoky tavern windows in an attempt to catch the idiosyncrasies of the Grandmas and the Veras.

This was all wonderful nonsense, of course. When Giles emerged from the three times-a-week journey into his imagination he didn't then go searching the back streets for characters to study, or sit disguised

"I told you a small open boat was false economy. We should have had the one with the cabin."

Daily Express, January 11th, 1968

Never could thoughts of summer and the open sea, here in wintry suburbia, be quite so inappropriate. How Giles loved to draw snow! Other artists always comment that the great skill in his snow scenes is his use of blank paper.

on a park bench examining ordinary people through a hole in a newspaper. Not a bit of it. As his cartoon was dispatched to the station he threw his brush into the air and skipped off to the nearest snug bar. There, rather than sit in a dark corner making notes, he would set the table on a roar and buy drinks for all. With his arm around a sturdy shoulder he would make merry until the last light had been extinguished, usually some hours after the drinking requirements of the law.

He would then make for home with a collection of those who had stood the pace and with his fellows, often caterwauling at the country moon, would tread an uncertain path to the farmhouse door. Within, wife Joan, in dressing gown, would cook sausages in a huge frying pan and the party would continue.

As the dawn tinted the eastern sky and as his chickens snuggled on their freshly laid eggs he could often be seen through the French windows with the last of the revellers, the stoutest heart of all, playing draughts.

On other days Giles would leap straight into his Jaguar XJ 120 and beat up the byways of Suffolk; go immediately from the studio to the estuary where he kept his ocean-going yacht, and sail the waters, from daylight to dusk, calling at waterside inns and treating all to the familiar Giles hospitality.

It was a favourite pastime of Giles's agitated employers to speak of his artistic need to be up in Suffolk with the people. To study. To moon about, as John Gordon put it. He undoubtedly drew richly from his adventures. Otherwise, it was poppycock, and in their hearts they knew it.

Much has been written here about Giles's grumpiness, his Grandma-like qualities. And this is true. Faced with the opposition and obstruction of life's irritations, frustrated by traffic wardens, tax inspectors, officious police constables, level-crossing keepers, politicians, bossy nursing sisters, weather forecasters and lazy workmen, he could be atrociously difficult. But when his spirit was free he was a man who could enjoy life like no other.

You could not expect such a man to put on a suit and catch a train to an office. In any case he didn't have to. Never did a newspaperman have such power over his employers. Never did an employee instil such fear and respect in those who filled his ever-expanding pay packet.

And never can a fellow have lived a life in such spectacular contrast to the existence of those who struggled to keep sane in that most famous of suburban households.

CHAPTER SIX

The Giles Family Christmas

In Gilesland Christmases are always white. The sky is invariably a heavy, leaden grey, and the corner of each windowpane is decorated with a little curve of freshly driven snow. Children with bright red noses and scarlet and yellow scarves hold up lanterns and – with mouths a perfect 'O' and eyes squeezed shut in apparently blissful innocence – sing their hearts out, uncomprehendingly calling upon the faithful, more often than not, with the Latin entreaty *Adeste fideles.*

Parson and vergers hurry about their business, bent against the bitter wind that scythes past churchyard gravestones and buffets the stained-glass angels above the church buttresses. The black branches of trees reach out cruelly like monsters in fairy tales, and the lights in windows are always bright yellow.

In Dickens's white Christmas, goodness always prevails. And it is here that the great novelist's concept of the yuletide festival parts company with that of Giles. For, as ever with our greatest cartoonist, mischief, misfortune, sabotage, anarchy and disruption tend to get the upper hand. What we know as the Christmas spirit, while struggling to make itself felt, more often than not loses the battle.

Father Christmas gets stuck in the chimney after raiding the brandy or, alternatively, is caught playing poker with a Guinness-swilling Grandma. He may just as likely be apprehended for speeding or be booked, reindeer and all, by a late, over-zealous Christmas Eve traffic warden exceeding his or her call of duty.

The mince pies will be flogged at half-price to the Salvation Army, and the turkey will probably be eaten by Butch. The kids will have transferred most of the labels on the Christmas presents under the tree in a manner designed to confuse and undermine thoroughly any goodwill which may have been evident, and they will have doubled the explosive charges in the crackers. Vera will be snuffling and sneezing with a cold which threatens to engulf the household.

It is at Christmas, especially, that the humour of Giles has always been at its most popular. Giles, in a sense, is most associated with Christmas.

His annuals, for example, have been paperback best-sellers – top of the list – since World War Two. His special Christmas cards, drawn initially for such charities as the Game Conservancy Trust and for the Royal National Lifeboat Institution and sold throughout the country and abroad, are always technicolour gems of glorious detail.

It is not just the dazzle of his draughtsmanship and his astonishing ability with snow and light that is so impressive; it is also his skill at producing a wonderfully Christmassy atmosphere by combining the magic with the ill-will, chaos and malevolence which is so often an essential underlying part of the festival. We love the romantic, magical idea of Christmas while recognising the domestic mayhem and misery which is so often the reality.

This is one of Giles's more celebrated Christmas cards. It was dedicated, with spectacular and only faintly distasteful irony, to the Royal National Institute for the Deaf. Giles supported many charities with his work. This one – as did all the artist's other good-hearted endeavours – raised a generous amount.

"We're parked on a double yellow line."

Daily Express, December 29th, 1970

The wonder of Giles snow! Three-quarters of this cartoon is blank paper. Giles admitted that in his entire life he found it difficult to remember a white Christmas. In much of the country, he believes, people just imagine that Christmases of childhood were blessed with a heavy fall of snow – an enduring but perfectly acceptable myth.

There are many favourite Giles Christmas cartoons, each collector having his own. One classic seasonal sketch, which was used commercially as a Christmas card, seems, however, to embody all the merriment and madness that brought such cheer to Giles's followers. We see most of the Family – Mother is doubtless at home doing the cooking – serenading what could well be Chiswick or some other area of outer London.

"Now for peace sake—don't tell the Missus we've had a drink."

Sunday Express, Dec. 27th, 1953

Giles is a sociable fellow, and once held his drink as well as any man. But he drew Christmas drunks with the sure hand of an artist who had bumped into more than one or two people – such as this impressively drawn group of revellers – who were unable to emulate his impressively disciplined style of enjoying himself.

Grandma is at the centre of the group, bawling her lungs out. The twins, airborne as usual, are lambasting a huge bass drum, young George has dispatched the triangle from its holder, George the bookworm is blasting out his contribution on a trombone which he has presumably dug out from the attic, Stinker is beating the cymbals and Butch is howling at the heavens. The carol, of course, is 'Silent Night'.

The card was drawn – appropriately – for the Royal National Institute for the Deaf.

In the picture the snow falls heavily in enormous, friendly flakes and it is very cold indeed. Distant, welcoming warmth is provided by the illuminated windows in houses and high-rise blocks. The sheer horror of the sound is reflected in the response of the local constable, holding up one hand as a command for the cacophony to cease and clutching the other to his ear.

174

"Dad, Mum says would you like a mince pie while we're waiting for the fire brigade?"

Daily Express, December 24th, 1979

Innocent little mites with the faces of angels sit by the fire. The true magic of that season never really stood a chance in this particular household. It is interesting to see that Stinker, the ever-prepared photographer, has acquired a rather magnificent vintage camera.

When Giles's wife Joan was asked why he created the Stinker character, she suggested that it was, perhaps, because he wanted to draw cameras. But the role of Stinker is probably rather more complex than that. Ever silent, he is usually about to capture on film that event which always follows the moment frozen in the cartoon. It is a pity we can't browse through Stinker's album.

"You say the lady kissed your head under the mistletoe thereby causing you sexual harassment?"

Daily Express, December 21st, 1982

Christmas mischief rather than overwhelming carnal desire must surely have been the reason for this ugly incident. However, it goes to show that the relatively new phrase in the sociological vernacular – sexual harassment – was already causing disruption even in 1982. Grandma under the mistletoe is a daunting thought.

176

"Don't fly off the handle, Grandma—we're only using your bed while our Christmas present's got flu."
Daily Express, December 30th, 1969

This is a fairly rare view of Grandma's bedroom. Her gallery of relatives always makes a fascinating study.

"I seem to remember a lot of brave talk this morning about not having a drink with the boys and coming home early to help us."

Daily Express, Dec. 24th, 1947

The most unhappy detail in this cartoon – crammed as it is with the richness of Giles's lunacy – is the fate of George the bookworm. He so seldom helps and when he does pick up a hammer, look what happens to the poor fellow.

It is a wonderful cartoon: Giles at his Christmas best.

The Giles Christmas as we know it, funnily enough, has little to do with the memories of Giles himself. He says: 'Actually, I can only remember it snowing over Christmas on one occasion. And that was on Christmas evening. White Christmases are a bit of a myth. We all imagine we remember them, but if we think about it, they never really happened.'

Nevertheless, it is the snow which gives the Giles Christmas its special quality. It is always freshly fallen and you feel you could put your hand into the picture and take a fistful of it, hold it by the fire and have it melt through your fingers. Some of Giles's Christmas scenes are so real that you feel, as you look at the cartoon, that a window has been opened and a bitter blast of air has caught you about the ears.

And yet, if it is studied, it becomes clear that all the snow in a Giles drawing is simply blank paper.

"They're signing a two-day truce with Grandma. They won't play any Christmas jokes on her if she promises she won't sing."

Daily Express, December 24th, 1968

An unholy pact!

Giles hasn't drawn snow; he has simply let it create itself. It is an effect which inspires wonderment even in his artist rivals.

Says Jak of the London *Evening Standard*, a marvellously funny cartoonist whose work, with its impressive sense of perspective and almost cinematic realism, owes a considerable amount to the example of Giles:

His winter scenes were bloody masterful. Some of his colour work – the sort of thing he used to do for the RNLI – were the achievements of a great painter. Amazing. Giles was a genius at what to leave out. His snow was simply an illusion created by untouched white paper. I always tend to overdraw and curse myself afterwards.

What they always say about Giles – especially in all those Christmas sketches, cartoons which I thought became a bit hackneyed – is how they laughed at the bits in the background. They say that to me sometimes. And my reaction is: 'Bugger the bits in the background. What about the bits in the foreground?' But you know what I really envy about Giles is his Family. I wish I had invented a bloody family. But I can't now, can I?

I always felt that Giles, in particular, was a marvellous Sunday newspaper cartoonist. His work was reflective and his style was leisurely. You could sort of settle down to one of his cartoons and enjoy it rather than expect to be served up with some pungent point of the week.

Jak, who is a lively, blunt, no-nonsense character, is surprisingly generous in his praise of Giles. They were rivals, in a sense, and there was a time when Jak was hoping that he might take over from the master on the *Daily Express*.

Jak makes no secret of the fact that he learned from the older artist and, in some respects, copied his technique. Although he would never have stolen an actual joke he was unwise enough, on one occasion, to have borrowed a particularly celebrated piece of professional mischief from Carl Giles. He had not taken into account the god-like reputation of his elder, which was such that Giles kept his employers in a constant state of anxiety over threatened defection.

Giles was able to cause the most terrible agitation amongst executives by his infrequent, and devastating, habit of half-hiding some obscene item

somewhere in the bustle of his pictures.

His favourite trick was to drop a packet of French letters in amongst the chaos, particularly when it involved American GIs, and hope to get it past those tormented men of the newspaper who had been instructed to vet every cartoon before it appeared in print.

Giles was victorious at least once and we reproduce here the wartime Christmas cartoon in which four of the little packets appear, carefully hidden.

'As a joke I thought I would do the same,' says Jak. 'You have got to remember that a French-letter packet in those days was an object of great obscenity. Anyway, it got through. Into the paper. There was a most terrible drama. The bosses at the paper were outraged and I received a half-page bollocking, which was full of phrases like "How dare you..." and "In future..."

'But the great Giles could get away with it, you see.'

One of Giles's greatest admirers is Michael Molloy, novelist and former editor-in-chief of Mirror Group Newspapers, whose early training was in art. Says Molloy:

We lived in a typical lower-middle-class home – a Giles home – and our house at Christmas time smelt of Rupert books and Giles annuals. You would look at a Giles Christmas cartoon, look at the chaos about you and say: 'How did he get in here? How did he know?' So much is going on in a Giles Christmas scene. It was not just full of independent detail, but everything that was happening was interrelated. It was connected and had a sense of movement. Grandma appears to be dozing by the fire as the kids light the fuse of a firework under her chair. Look again and you can see that Grandma has one eye open and that her hand is just about to

"Just like it said in the invite, Tex—'Widow and five single daughters would like to entertain party of American soldiers for Christmas'."

Four tiny packets of French letters are concealed in this cartoon. Giles's editor failed to spot them, but they're clearly there.

"Hold it, Dad—Auntie Ivy hasn't quite gone yet."

Daily Express, December 28th, 1967

When you've seen Auntie Ivy, Grandma becomes Mother Theresa!

reach for the poker. The cat is about to jump up at a decoration and you can see that the chain reaction which will follow will probably bring the whole tree down on Vera, who has her head under a towel inhaling some cold cure out of a steaming bowl.

182

"I like the way they always ask you if you'd LIKE to help them with the decorations."

Sunday Express, December 20th, 1959

This is another pet irritation of Giles's, something which has often been expressed at his Suffolk farm. It is the idea of a woman asking a well-settled and relaxed man, usually happily slumbering before the television set, if he would 'like' to help. Obviously, if he did (you can see Giles reasoning in his inimitably grumpy manner), he would have been up and helping, like mad. Those who know Giles will see, not Father here, but Carl himself.

"Right—on the show of hands Sebastian gets a reprieve—one of you go to the shop and get six large tins of corned beef."

Sunday Express, December 17th, 1978

Fatal to give them a name, of course.

Such an effect is the result of Giles's early teenage training as an animator for the great film-maker, Alexander Korda. Giles himself once explained that he saw his cartoons merely as 'still' frames in a moving sequence. He would imagine the complex action in his head and suddenly, at just the right moment, shout 'stop'. He would then draw what he saw.

'His cartoons display animating genius,' says Molloy. 'Giles works like a camera. But what made his Christmas cartoons so special was that they showed the strength of the Family. They depicted the antithesis of loneliness. Despite the chaos and the anarchy there was a wonderful sense of security, of warmth and of belonging. There was snow outside the window, a fire in the hearth and the tree was lit up and festooned with bunting. What more could you want?'

There was also, perhaps, a strong feeling of nostalgia in Giles's Christmas art. Almost a bitter-sweet quality, a sadness for unrecoverable innocence. Says Giles:

Although we didn't have white Christmases, they were wonderful, very special times in our home. We had huge numbers of presents, I remember. This was because my father used to bring them all from his shop. Trains, little lorries, all kinds of things. Because he was a tobacconist, he had all these samples which showed the customer what he would be able to swap for a collection of cigarette cards. So many cards would get you a lorry, a large number of cards would get you something very special. We had stockings and pillowcases full of gifts.

It was the trains I remember more than anything else. People forget now, but in those days of steam the engines were brightly coloured and shiny. The locomotives on LNER – that was London-North Eastern – were green, with wonderful scarlet wheels. And a red bumper. If you came from my kind of family you would have an LNER train set. If you lived in a rich family your train would probably be GWR – that was the Great Western. Posh people used the Great Western – to go to places like the races at Cheltenham. GWR livery was brown and yellow. If you look at some of the small stations along the old Great Western routes you can still see the benches, still kept freshly painted in the old colours.

Oh, you all wanted to be engine drivers ... Of course, we lived in an area where all the great stations were and engine drivers used to come into my father's shop for their tobacco. They all wore caps and smoked pipes. There was always that lovely smell about them. I remember one of the drivers who was ever such a nice man – I went round one Christmas and my father held me up to him so that I could shake his hand.

Such are the vivid Christmas recollections of any childhood. But what is special about the recollections of Carl Giles is their clarity.

'My brother gave me a fort for Christmas once,' he says. 'It came with lead soldiers and farm animals. They were made, I remember, by Brittans, the famous London toy manufacturers. The red guardsmen always had one arm which moved. You could make them march or shoulder their rifles.'

If you look around Giles's neat and brightly painted farmhouse outside Ipswich you will see these toys, still there. On the windowsill there are Dinky fire engines and newspaper delivery vans, little steam locomotives and 1920s buses.

"'George,' I said, 'Christmas Eve. What better time to ask our new neighbours round for a drink and meet Mummy'."

Daily Express, December 24th, 1974

The full madness of it all.

"Christmas comes but once a year—another fort for me and another doll's cradle for you."

Sunday Express, December 8th, 1985

Giles recalls his own Christmases with great affection. He remembers the joy at receiving train sets in the bright scarlet and green colours of LNER – the London-North Eastern Railway. 'Kids of rich families,' he says, 'would get GWR train sets – that was the Great Western, which took you to places like the races at Cheltenham. But what I remember at Christmas were the forts and the lead soldiers – guardsmen who had one arm that moved.'

This cartoon, for all of its fun, shows Giles in nostalgic mood. Suddenly that chaotic shed in the garden has become the quiet and well-ordered place of a craftsman. Giles himself, indeed.

"Grandma's been a great help. She's packed all the presents but forgot to label them which one's which."

Sunday Express, December 18th, 1983

We've all done it!

"Mum! Dad's just given the carol singers a cheque for five million pounds."

Sunday Express, December 23rd, 1962

Informer!

Olly O!!

all creatures great and small.

mr giles Christmas aunts arriving

When they asked Mr. Giles how he was going to spend Christmas, he said: "No comment." So as I expect this one will be exactly the

head aunt

same as all his other 100-odd Christmases here is this Christmas forecast. First thing he does is to round up all his aunts nephews and neices and their aunts nephews and nieces etc. And bring them all to the house in one go in a cattle float. Coming from a jockey family they're not very high. And all walk under the table without bending down and put their hats on a chair.

They're the same little black hats and coats they had when Mr. Giles was four.

And I once got a thick Christmas ear for saying they look like a flock of little rooks (not the Jean version). They have a very happy festive season sitting round the fire humming of wintergreen ointment and embrocation. And chatting ailments.

Ollyfied mr giles

↑ my joke!

Finally, a word about it all from Giles Junior.

And making whispers about Mr. Giles' habits which you can hear half a mile away. His head aunt keeps looking in his direction shaking her head and saying: "Pity." Mr. Giles is never very happy the rest of the year, but Christmas Aunt time he's 10 times worse.

His Head Aunt says the only way he and his mates could make Christmas different to the rest of the year would be for them to go on the wagon.

He got very jumpy when the paper told him his old mate Jean-Ground-Glass-and-Acid was coming down to write a piece about him and Christmas. He worked out a rota for us all to go out and buy every edition it was in throughout the land. But I think Jean Rook is very nice and wouldn't half have given him a dusting. Ah, well, it only comes once a year —and I expect the New Year will be worse. Merry Easter.

P.S. Vera's got her Christmas cold which usually lasts till next Christmas.

        Noel.

Daily Express, December 24th, 1973

Everywhere there are games: football games and board games and card games. The house is a place where childhood has been suspended. There are no youngsters about. Giles has no children. His is a house full of his own childhood. Indeed, it is one of the secrets of the genius of Carl Giles that he has never grown old.

It is sad too. For looking at him in his wheelchair, his sight failing, his hands too weak to draw, one feels that he is constantly puzzled over where it has all gone – and so quickly.

What makes memories of Christmas almost unique for Carl Giles and his wife is that they are first cousins. They were an enormously close family, all living near one another in the Islington and King's Cross area of London. All the aunts and at least one set of the grandparents would gather and there would be the trio of young Carl, sister Eileen – ever fearful for the fate of her toys – and cousin Joan.

Who could have told in those faraway Christmas gatherings that Carl and Joan would one day be man and wife? The notion may well have been regarded with horror.

Carl and Joan, unlike most married couples, have literally shared their whole life. Their first memories together were of Christmas. Even now, sixty-five years on and more, Carl, cousin Joan and sister Eileen still gather for the festival. There is a tree, there is the bunting, there are presents and there is still the laughter.

And there is Butch, by the fire, one eye opening sleepily at the sound of his master's voice. Butch is the common denominator between the Giles's real world and that which exists within the frame of a Giles cartoon. With the licence of a special magic he wanders between these two realms. One moment he is in the actual Giles farmhouse outside Ipswich, faintly puzzled by the festive rituals that surround him; the next he is under Grandma's chair. Vera is sniffing in a corner, the girls are decorating the tree and an evil child is pushing holly into a pair of bedroom slippers.

You might almost expect the distant, though firm cry of 'Butch, c'mere' and to see the creature, long-suffering like his mistress and never quite sure of his place in the world, to stagger to his feet and lope out of the picture into his other favoured position in that Suffolk sitting room. Perhaps, when we're not looking, that's exactly what happens. It's fun to imagine so, in any case.

Such is the enchantment of Giles.